Y0-CBV-521

Philadelphia
MAGAZINE'S

Best
of **Philly**™
The Ultimate Guide

**Where to find the best food, shopping,
culture, and fun in the Delaware Valley**

by Janet Bukovinsky Teacher

RUNNING PRESS
PHILADELPHIA · LONDON

Acknowledgments

Thanks to the past and present editorial staff of *Philadelphia Magazine*—including, but not limited to, Eliot Kaplan, Stephen Fried, Lisa DePaulo, Amy Donohue, Ronnie Polaneczky, Lou Harry and Larry Platt, with research assistance by Beth Kwon.

Canadian representatives: General Publishing Co., Ltd., 30 Lesmill Road, Don Mills, Ontario M3B 2T6.

9 8 7 6 5 4 3 2 1
Digit on the right indicates the number of this printing.

Library of Congress Cataloging-in-Publication Number 94–67760

ISBN 1–56138–479–8

Cover design by Toby Schmidt
Front cover: Philadelphia skyline by Seymour Mednick,
   pretzel by Craig DeMartino
Back cover: Mayor Ed Rendell by Jim Graham/GSI
Interior design by Paul Kepple
Interior illustrations by William Waitzman
Photo Research by Susan Oyama
Typeset in Universe and Bodoni

This book may be ordered by mail from the publisher.
Please add $2.50 for postage and handling.
But try your bookstore first!

Running Press Book Publishers
125 South Twenty-second Street
Philadelphia, Pennsylvania 19103–4399

Contents

Introduction

"God couldn't be here tonight, so we've taken this opportunity to fill in for him."

Thus began the very first "Best of Philly™" article in *Philadelphia Magazine*, back in May, 1974. With monumental chutzpah and typical '70's in-your-face attitude, the magazine's editors put together a feature composed of their own highly subjective opinions on local restaurants, bars, politics and city life. Little did they know they were coming up with a formula that would be knocked off, for decades to come, in every regional publication from *Honolulu* to *Pittsburgh*.

Local loremeisters long believed that Philly Mag was the first of the city magazines out of the gate with the "Best of" concept, but the truth is that the notion was born in Boston. Geoffrey Precourt, then editor of *Boston Magazine*, the sister publication of *Philadelphia*, came up with the idea when a last-minute dispute left him with just four days to devise a meaty cover story for his April issue. Maury Z. Levy, then editorial director of *Philadelphia*, happened to be in the *Boston* offices, looking over Precourt's shoulder. Levy brought the idea—at that time, a compendium of not just the best, but also the worst—to Philly, and ran with it in a frank, opinionated direction.

Back then, the methodology used for determining the best of the city's offerings was hardly scientific. The magazine's editors polled their friends—"Hey, where's the best hoagie?"—and then followed up by visiting for a taste-test of each candidate's fare. According to Levy, the article was meant to be just a one-time event, a playful exercise in the spirit of fun.

But an odd thing happened when the issue hit the newsstands—Philadelphians took it seriously. Levy and his staffers observed an unsettling phenomenon, a tradition in the making: people on the street were using the issue as a sort of guidebook, obediently having dinner at the "best" Chinese restaurant followed by two scoops of lemon at the "best" water ice stand.

Meanwhile the magazine's editorial offices were inundated with huffy phone calls and letters ("How dare you say that So-and-So's is the best? *I* know where the best one is!"). Food samples started showing up at the receptionist's desk, dropped

off by representatives from establishments claim-
ing to make a better pretzel, hoagie, cheesesteak,
brownie, whatever. A star was born—or maybe a
monster. From then on, we couldn't *not* do a Best
of Philly™. In a city legendary for its contentious-
ness, deserved or not, people loved the whole
superlative thing, and even more, loved to dis-
agree with it.

Because it appeared that the reputations of certain establishments were made or broken based on
Best of Philly™ recommendations they did or didn't
receive, the editors gradually began treating the
annual article with more consideration. Food tastings were organized, to which local bigwigs and
celebrities were invited for the purpose of casting
their votes. Over the years, the tasting concept
went beyond food to events like a "clipathon" in
which hair designers competed for audience
approval, using volunteer heads as their medium.
There were battles of the bands—from hard rock
to reggae—as well as stand-up comic joke-offs,
magician trick-offs, and in 1988, a gathering of
city magazine editors from all across the country
who flew into town to help pick the best landmark.
(Hint: They hated the Rocky statue.) Food tastings escalated in grandiosity: there was the dessert
cart parade down Walnut Street, the marathon
pizza relay (120, count 'em, 120 pies!) at Franklin
Mills Mall, and the night a self-indulgent claque

of editors rode around in a limo trying to find the best martini.

Today, how are these decisions made? There's no pat answer, for each category is different. The bottom line is that every Best of Philly™ is a team effort. All year, our writers and editors shop for, taste and sample countless goodies. They visit interesting places and make note of what they see. But in the end, it's still unabashedly subjective, and comes down to the preferences and prejudices of a group of human beings whose job it is to observe the city. Therefore, what we deem the best pizza may not please you if we like thin crust and you prefer thick. All we can guarantee is that our pizza will be pretty damn good, because we've got the research—and bulging bellies—to back it up.

Twenty-something years after that first Best of Philly™, we're taking this thing seriously enough that we can personally attest to the validity of every entry—at least at the time it was written. All of the information contained herein was current at press time, but keep in mind that some of the establishments may have closed, moved or been renamed since then. We're also doing our best to make Best of Philly™ relevant to *all* segments of the Philadelphia area by picking regional champions in the critical categories of cheesesteaks, hoagies, pizzas and milkshakes—in the event that you live on the Main Line, and can't drive to South Philly every time the urge for chocolate water ice strikes.

Some aspects of Best of Philly™, however, haven't changed a bit: it's still meant to be fun, enlightening and sometimes obnoxiously opinionated. That's our prerogative, and you don't have to agree with everything. In fact, you won't. Such shameless subjectivity has made "Best of Philly™" the top-selling issue of *Philadelphia Magazine*, the one that residents and tourists alike hang onto for ideas on where to go and what to do with their precious free moments and discretionary good-time cash. This book was compiled in the same spirit, with honest disclosures on what we think is worthwhile *and* what's disappointing. Philly is a city blessed with hundreds of bona fide "bests"—more than enough to fill the covers of an entire book, we realized recently. So as the magazine's Senior Writer, restaurant reviewer and survivor of a quadrillion slices of potential Best of Philly™ pizzas, I finally sat down and did just that.

—*Janet Bukovinsky Teacher*

CHAPTER ONE

Destinations and Celebrations:
Public Philadelphia

Physically, Philly is an amiable, accessible city: our north-to-south cross streets are numbered, our boundaries are bordered with water and our architecture, much of it strikingly well preserved, spans the last three centuries, with technology ranging from hand-cast bricks to dazzling steel. It's also a city for walking, as handsomely endowed with public artworks as with the quirky vestiges of real life that bespeak the creativity of the human imagination.

City Sites

ARCHITECTURAL LANDMARK: The true distinguishing spire of the city skyline, with its gentle red glow, is the **Philadelphia Saving Fund Society**, or **PSFS**, building. Designed by Philadelphian George Howe and Swiss architect William Lescaze, it was completed in 1932, a gleam of prosperity in the Great Depression, to the tune of $8 million. One of the first buildings with air conditioning, it is also among the country's most beautifully maintained examples of the International style of architecture—the first skyscrapers (12 South 12th Street).

ARCHITECTURAL MASTERPIECE, NEW: Helmut Jahn's **One Liberty Place** pierces the Philly skyline with a proud spire as grand as Manhattan's Empire State Building. The airy mall and food court on ground level are worth a look, but try to get yourself invited to an office on one of the top floors for a stupendous vista onto the city and beyond (17th and Market Streets).

ARCHITECTURAL MASTERPIECE, OLD: When construction was completed in 1876, comparisons were instantly made to the Louvre. Today, the **Pennsylvania Academy of the Fine Arts**, perhaps the finest of numerous buildings designed by "Fearless Frank" Furness, remains the city's proudest Victorian edifice. Inside see 300 years of American art, including works inside by Thomas Eakins and Alexander Calder, both of whom taught here (Broad and Cherry Streets).

> The Victorian edifice of the country's first art museum, the Museum of American Art of the Pennsylvania Academy of the Fine Arts, is an exhibit in itself.

ARCHITECTURAL QUIRK: The **trinity house**, also known as the "Father, Son and Holy Ghost," "faith, hope and charity" or the "high-hat." Cozy, three-room row homes built in the eighteenth and nineteenth centuries, they typically feature

three square or rectangular rooms set atop each other, with a connecting staircase. The best streets to see them are Elfreth's Alley—a national landmark dating back to the 1720s—and further uptown, on the 1900 block of Waverly Street.

BIG BELL: No, not *that* one. The **Founder's Bell** inside the Philadelphia National Bank in Old City rings the hours from 9 a.m. to 9 p.m. except Sundays and holidays. Bigger by a ton than the Liberty Bell, it was commissioned in 1926 by Rodman Wanamaker to mark the 50th anniversary of his family's department store. Musicians say it has a tone of almost perfect clarity (Chestnut and Broad Streets).

BIRD'S-EYE VIEW OF PHILLY: From the air, during a Friday-at-dusk ride by **Sterling Helicopter**. These thrilling chopper excursions whisk you over the Ben Franklin Bridge, over the skyline, past the Zoo and back to earth. Last flight is at 5:45 p.m. (Delaware Avenue and Catharine Street, 271-2510).

CIVIC GESTURE: Closing **West River Drive** to automobile traffic every weekend from sunrise to sunset so bicycle riders and pedestrians can take to the street—*all* of the street.

CITY VIEW: From the **Spring Garden Bridge**, at sunup or sunset, when the sky is colored that otherworldly pearlescent violet. A show worthy of its own soundtrack.

DOORS: The sacred scarlet portals on medieval-Gothic **St. Mark's Church.** Replete with swirling wrought iron (look closely to find the tiny, animated faces), they're the work of nineteenth-century Philadelphia iron artisan Samuel Yellin (1625 Locust Street).

Welcome to Philly! Make an unforgettable entrance, day or night, via the magnificent Ben Franklin Bridge.

ELECTRONIC MESSAGES: Center Cityites scan the skyline to read that digital bulletin board flashing across the top four floors of the **Philadelphia Electric Company (PECO)** building. It transmits nearly 2,000 messages a year via 2,800 70-watt lights. Posting an announcement costs only $15 a night, but although PECO gets many requests for marriage proposals, they only consider messages of worthwhile community events (2301 Market Street).

GARGOYLES: Atop the **Drake Tower**, which in its former life was a hotel frequented by distinguished Broadway actors passing through Philly for pre-Manhattan tryouts. Now it's an apartment building (1512 Spruce Street).

GATEWAY TO PHILLY: Across the 800,000-ton, $37 million, robin's-egg-blue **Ben Franklin Bridge**—lit to twinkly perfection for America's Bicentennial by an architect from the world-class local firm Venturi, Scott Brown and Associates.

GREAT BIG THING THAT FINALLY GOT FINISHED: The **Blue Route**, a.k.a. Route 476, the highway that introduced lower Delaware County to the rest of the world.

ICON: The rust-red, 45-foot-high domestic icon by sculptor Claes Oldenburg known as the **Clothespin** was given to the city in 1976 by developer Jack Wolgin. Since then, it's anchored the plaza and subway entrance between the twin towers of Wolgin's Centre Square complex (15th and Market Streets).

NEON, INDOOR: The ranks of saluting swabbies and bright blue waves at the **U.S. Navy Recruiting Center** (123 North Broad Street).

NEON, OUTDOOR: Bright red and stylishly angular, atop the **Philadelphia Arts Bank**, a multi-use rental facility and performance space. The sign has become a beacon on Center City's fledgling Avenue of the Arts (601 South Broad Street, 545–0590).

NEW ATTRACTION: The dazzling **Philadelphia Convention Center**. Don't wait until an interesting trade show comes to town—it's worth entering the florid-carpeted lobby (open 9 a.m. to 5 p.m. daily) to view what is arguably Philadelphia's best collection of work by contemporary local artists, including Sidney Goodman and Bo Bartlett. But do try to get yourself invited to a party in the immense Train Shed Ballroom, too (1101 Arch Street, 418–4700).

OUTSIDER ARTISTS: Look for colorful, upbeat murals produced by members and volunteers of the **Philadelphia Anti-Graffiti Network** on exterior walls throughout the city—particularly in Fairmount, North Philly and West Philly. Its cheerful, Rousseau-esque jungle panorama at 6th and South has transformed a mundane McDonald's into a destination for connoisseurs of alfresco art (686–1550).

PROPOSED PUBLIC PROJECT: Converting the gorgeous, Roman-temple style **Fairmount Waterworks**, completed in 1815, into a multi-use, athletic-entertainment facility. Now that it looks as though the Kelly Drive bike path will be extended

Hang out under Oldenburg's Clothespin near City Hall.

The Arts Bank lights up Philly's fledgling Avenue of the Arts.

along the Schuylkill to Spruce Street, this site near 25th Street is prime for a happening.

REASON TO HANG OUT IN CENTER CITY ON WEDNESDAYS: A few places, namely Borders Book Shop, stay open until 10 p.m. every night of the week. But Wednesday is **"Make It A Night"** time in Center City, when many stores keep mall hours, many restaurants offer special deals and downtown Philadelphia shines in the dark.

REASON TO TAKE AMTRAK: Sure, the trains mostly run on time these days. But the real reason is **30th Street Station**, the country's first major depot designed for those newfangled electric trains. On the National Register of Historic Places, it was finished in 1934 and recently restored—relit, repainted, bronze elevator doors buffed, the works. You saw it in *Witness* and *Trading Places*, and in person, it still captivates an audience, from the tragic, winged Pennsylvania Railroad War Memorial statue to the ornately coffered ceilings (30th Street and John F. Kennedy Blvd.).

SEASONAL TREAT FOR GARDEN VOYEURS: The Philadelphia Art Museum's popular springtime tour of **Historic Houses in Flower** takes you through Fairmount Park jewels with enticing names like Lemon Hill and Strawberry Mansion at the height of blooming season (684–7926).

SEASONAL TREAT FOR HOUSE VOYEURS: **Philadelphia Open House**, a series of tours through Rittenhouse Square, Old City, Society Hill, the Main Line and Bucks County, with trips to William Penn's estate, Pennsbury, and the Biddles' Andalusia (928–1188).

SIGN OF SPRING, CITY: Plumes of water begin arching out of the **Swann Memorial Fountain**, designed by estimable Philadelphia sculptor Alexander Stirling Calder and completed in 1924 for the Parkway's Logan Square.

Getting Around:

Transportation Tips and Touts

ALTERNATIVE TRANSPORTATION: Is that a wayward grape with turquoise wings? No, it's the purple bus known as **Phlash**, the city's response to the federal Clean Cities program which encourages the use of alternative fuel vehicles. More to the point, it's a convenient downtown-to-waterfront bus loop operating Monday through Saturday from 10 a.m. to midnight (Call 4–PHLASH for rates and routes).

BUS: The goofily named **Ben Frankline** (Route 76) lurches up Walnut to 5th Street, over to Market, past City Hall and down to the Art Museum on JFK Blvd. It's quick, uncrowded and only 50 cents. The reason it's so much better than regular SEPTA? It's meant for tourists, not for those of us who really live here.

CAB COMPANY: **Olde City Taxi** has a higher-than-average percentage of clean cabs and courteous drivers. Just be aware of that old-timer's ploy when the driver asks you how much your ride *usually* costs, and then turns off the meter (338–0838).

PUBLIC TRANSPORTATION TO PENN OR DELAWARE AVENUE:
As much as people rail against SEPTA, our local transportation authority, it does a good job of getting you where you want to go. Take the **Blue Line**, a.k.a. "The Frankford El," to the University of Pennsylvania or Drexel, as well as to Penn's Landing or the Delaware Avenue nightclubs.

PUBLIC TRANSPORTATION TO THE VET: The **Orange Line**, a.k.a. "The Broad Street Line," follows Broad Street north to south. Take this to LaSalle or Temple universities, and to the Spectrum, Veterans Stadium and South Philly.

THING FOR TOURISTS TO COMPLAIN ABOUT: Most of our cabs, frankly, are jouncing, jostling ashtrays on bald tires with no suspension, propelled by drivers who summon up their best English to ask you directions to the destination you've just told them while the meter ticks to $1.80, the starting fare. Should this happen, scream for the driver to stop and get out with all due outrage to hail another cab.

WAY TO GO ALL OVER THE PLACE IN ONE DAY: SEPTA's DayPass provides 24 hours unlimited riding on all city transit plus one-way passage on the efficient Airport Line, for $5. Buy tickets at the Visitors Center, 16th Street and JFK Blvd. (Call 580–7777 for information).

WAY TO GET AROUND PHILLY: Walk. Laid out in a precise grid by a surveyor for William Penn in the 17th century, the numbered streets run north to south and those with names run east to west. Even a newcomer can keep that straight.

Catch a ride on SEPTA's Chestnut Hill Trolley.

SIGN OF SPRING, ON YOUR WAY OUT OF THE CITY: Early-morning scullers skimming the surface of the Schuylkill (say that three times fast!) in front of **Boathouse Row**.

SIGN OF SUMMER, CITY: The Catholic schoolgirls of **John W. Hallahan High School** frolicking in the fountains at Logan Square and JFK Plaza. Not condoned by the nuns in charge, but enough of a tradition that the mayor's office makes sure there's clean water in the fountains just for the occasion.

USE OF TAX DOLLARS: The Philadelphia prison system's **Hospitality Apprenticeship Program**, a.k.a. the Hard Time Cafe. By turning cons into culinary virtuosos, HAP puts them to work in the kitchen, feeding each other while they're in the can and—more importantly—once they're out.

VESTIGE OF GRANDEUR IN FAIRMOUNT PARK: Once, it housed the Statue of Liberty's hand gripping the torch, but now **Memorial Hall** is the home of the Fairmount Park Commission. Of the five monumental exhibition halls built for America's Centennial Exposition of 1876, it's the only one still standing. Designed by German immigrant Hermann J. Schwarzmann, this Renaissance-style confection, gingerbready and ornate, can be rented for special events (Call 685–0000 for information).

VIEW OF THE DELAWARE, FISHEYE: From aboard the **River Bus** ferry connecting the Philadelphia and Camden riverfronts. The 10-minute crossing provides a refreshing view of both cities. Pick it up (between May 15 and September 15) outside the Port of History Museum at Philly's Penn's Landing or the New Jersey State Aquarium in Camden.

Historical Philly:
The Footprints of Time

Walk where the signers of the Declaration of Independence walked. See, up close, the Liberty Bell, which tolled to mark the first public reading of that document. Tread upon the floorboards where Betsy Ross stitched a flag, if not *the* flag. Many of Philly's historic landmarks are found in Independence National Historic Park, a 46-acre enclave of 40-plus buildings occupying all or parts of 16 city blocks. Typically, many Philadelphians have never made the trek down here, although the sneakered feet of 1.5 million visitors pass through every year.

APPRECIATION OF BENJAMIN FRANKLIN: Isamu Noguchi's masterful 101-foot-tall sculpture of stainless steel, entitled **Bolt of Lightning** (North 5th and Vine Streets).

IMPERSONATION OF BENJAMIN FRANKLIN, IN THE FLESH: Two highly competitive Philadelphians make their livings by sporting knickers and tiny glasses, holding forth in the myriad sayings of the "American Da Vinci" and are constantly taunted by tourists at Independence National Historical Park to "Go fly a kite!" Our vote for the better Ben is **Ralph Archbold**.

IMPERSONATION OF BENJAMIN FRANKLIN, ON FILM: Eli Wallach, who appears in the 28-minute film *Independence*, shown a dozen times each day, free of charge, in the Visitor's Center (South 3rd Street between Chestnut and Walnut, 597–8974).

IMPERSONATION OF A CASH MACHINE: In the Visitor's Center, while waiting for the next showing of *Independence*, stroll through the **Constitution** exhibit. TV screens are set up with interactive displays ("If you want to hear about abortion, press this box") which lead you through an intricate maze of videotaped mini-segments.

PLACE TO EAT AS OUR FOUNDING FATHERS DID: **City Tavern**, the place where Paul Revere galloped up with the news that the British had closed Boston Harbor. Recently reopened after a 27-year reconstruction (and you think *your* contractor works slowly!), the handsome taproom-dining room has a menu daunting in its historically authentic heft (Walnut and South 2nd Streets, 413–1443).

TRADE ORGANIZATION WITH A MISSION: Other than making more money for themselves, that is. The **Carpenters' Company** consists of more than 100 builders, engineers and architects actively engaged in the construction industry in and around Philadelphia. Their primary mission is the preservation of Carpenters' Hall, built in 1774, where the Continental Congress met for the first time ever (320 Chestnut Street).

REASONS TO MAKE A RESERVATION FOR A GUIDED TOUR: The only two places in the park which require reservations are **Bishop White House** (a 1787 gem featuring a wine cellar, ice pit and root cellar) and the **Dilworth-Todd-Moylan House** (the first marriage home of Dolly Madison). And if you have any interest in antiques, both are well worth exploring with a tour guide (South 3rd Street between Chestnut and Walnut Streets, 597–8974).

SOUVENIR-BUYING STRATEGY: For true souvenir aficionados, the kitschier the better. Collectors of the most gleefully tacky mementoes of Independence National Historical Park—miniature Liberty Bells, snow globes and the like—should head for **Xenos Candy and Gifts** (231 Chestnut Street, 922–1445).

PLACE TO SIT AND REST: Amid the historical splendor of the Park is a modest patch of fenced-in yard with an old pump and a restoration of a typical workman's family home from the time of the Revolution. Park yourself on one of the benches near this **Eighteenth Century Garden**, where in summer, corn and cherry tomatoes flourish in the sun (South 4th Street between Walnut and Chestnut Streets).

Frankly, sometimes it's hard to tell who's who in historical Philadelphia. Here, Ralph Archbold poses as the 20th-century Benjamin Franklin.

Franklin Court, with its underground museum and exhibits, stands on the site of Ben Franklin's home.

Join the camera-wielding hordes at Independence Hall, the birthplace of the nation.

RESTROOM NEAR THE LIBERTY BELL: As long as you're not touring with a motley crew or a passel of unruly children, summon up your best attitude and sashay past the doormen into the Omni Hotel at **Independence Square**, where the restrooms are enormously restful and clean, with niceties like cloth hand towels (401 Chestnut Street).

BUILDING THAT ISN'T THERE: Since the house where Benjamin Franklin lived didn't survive the centuries, the National Park Service commissioned world-renowned Philadelphia architects Venturi, Scott Brown and Associates to create an "interpretive complex" at **Franklin Court**. Their timelessly intriguing skeleton of a house is a pleasing bit of modernity amidst the elderly splendors of the Park (312–22 Market Street).

MURAL: The **Dream Garden**, Louis Comfort Tiffany's 49-foot-long glass mosaic in the lobby of the magnificently restored **Curtis Center** is a luminous translation of Maxfield Parrish's work. Commissioned by the Curtis Publishing Institute in 1911, the mosaic is perhaps the finest Tiffany mural in the world (Independence Square West, 238–6450).

The Liberty Bell Pavilion allows 24-hour viewing of this historic icon.

Best Fetes:
The Year in Special Events and Festivals

The Mummers' spectacular parade heralds a memorable New Year.

JANUARY's hottest show is the annual **Mummers Parade** to City Hall, a beery, hokey, uniquely Philly event that leaves the Center City route littered with sequins, feathers and other flashy detritus from these beloved string bands. In **FEBRUARY/MARCH**, roses bloom months ahead of nature's schedule at the nationally renowned **Philadelphia Flower Show** (625–8250). **APRIL** brings the **Penn Relays** to the University of Pennsylvania's Franklin Field, with the opportunity to see young track stars in the making, as well as world-famous Olympians (898–6121). That same month sees the culinary gathering which has put Philly on the country's food map: **The Book & the Cook**, in which cookbook authors and accomplished chefs from around the world come to town for special dinners at scores of city restaurants (686–3662). Come **MAY**, it's a Memorial Day

"Last call for the Penn Relays Carnival!" Don't miss the world's oldest and largest track and field meet in April. Here Rich Kenah of Georgetown leans for a win in 1981.

Plush rooms of blooms at the annual Philadelphia Flower Show.

tradition to take in some of the **Jambalaya Jam**, where zydeco-Cajun-Creole bands take the stand and crawfish heads are sucked with abandon down on the waterfront at Penn's Landing (336–2000).

Party New-Orleans style at Jambalaya Jam, the June music festival at Penn's Landing.

JUNE is a party in the funky riverside neighborhood of Manayunk, which hosts both the **Manayunk Arts Festival** and the **CoreStates Cycling Championship**; the latter continues to thrill onlookers who can't for the life of them figure out how those bikers *pedal* up those wicked Manayunk hills, especially The Wall (973–3546). June is also time for the **Mellon/PSFS Jazz Festival** at the Valley Forge Music Fair (829–9233), and the slice-of-preppy-life **Horse and Pony Show at Devon** (Devon Fairgrounds, Lancaster Avenue, Devon, 610–296–8668). In early **SEPTEMBER**, the hottest ticket in town is to the **Best of Philly™** party, a showplace for the food, entertainment and people who garner those annual awards from *Philadelphia Magazine* (564–7700). **OCTOBER** brings **Taste the Harvest**, a celebration of the superb foods grown and produced in our region, from heirloom vegetables to organically certified duck (686–3662). In **NOVEMBER** and **DECEMBER**, the best and brightest sight in town is the spectacular light show inside the **John Wanamaker** department store—a must-see for starry-eyed kids and romantics of all ages (422–2000).

CHAPTER TWO

Delicious Philly:
The Food that Makes Us Special

Philadelphia is a mouth that roars—for indigenous specialties like cheesesteaks, soft pretzels and hoagies, as well as for spicy Italian cooking, the hautest French and the hippest barbecue. Those with pronounced ethnic tastes are in the right place too—we've got Burmese, Vietnamese, African and more tasty versions of fusion cuisine than you can shake a chopstick at.

....

Good Mornings

ALL-YOU-CAN-EAT BRUNCH, MODEST: Sunday morning brings out the art lovers and the wildly hungry, good-looking student crowd at the **Art Museum** for its bountiful, beautifully presented $15 brunch (Benjamin Franklin Parkway, 763–8100).

ALL-YOU-CAN-EAT BRUNCH, GRAND: The scrupulously well-tended Sunday-best buffet at the **Fountain** in the Four Seasons Hotel is *the* place to celebrate family occasions—or the peaceful lack thereof (1 Logan Square, North 18th and Benjamin Franklin Parkway, 963–1500).

BREAKFAST, COUNTRIFIED: Flannel-soft buttermilk biscuits, buttered hot grits, eggs done just so and other humble ways to start the day are on the menu at good-old-boy chef Jack McDavid's **Down Home Grill** (1800 Spring Garden Street, 557–7510).

BREAKFAST, CITIFIED: "Jumbot" omelet stuffed with Italian sausage, cheese, potatoes, onions and peppers, at the sprightly new **Emil's**, which, for 50 years, was the depressing old Emil's, until it closed for major renovation last summer (1800 South Broad Street, 468–4474).

BREAKFAST, MAIN LINE: Scrambled eggs, white toast and preppy-watching at tidy **Minella's Diner**, a diner-car vision in vintage quilted stainless steel (320 Lancaster Avenue, Wayne, 610–687–1575).

BREAKFAST TREAT: Sausage, egg and cheese strombolis from **Philadelphia Stromboli Company**. Cholesterol on the run (15th and Sansom streets, 568–3777; 11th and Walnut Streets, 351–1156).

BRUNCH, LAID-BACK: The glorious muffins at mellow **Le Bus** in Manayunk are straight from the oven, and the seven-grain flapjacks are improbably light (4266 Main Street, 487–2663).

BRUNCH, SEE-AND-BE-SEEN, 'BURBS: The Volvo-wagon set flocks in their polo shirts and discreet pearls to sunny, casual **Carolina's Restaurant & Bar**, where the classical music and classic menu put everyone at ease (333 Belrose Lane, Radnor, 610–293–1000).

BRUNCH, SEE-AND-BE-SEEN, CITY: Well, they don't call it brunch at grimy **Famous Deli**, but that's what it is when you can linger for hours with your lox and bagel and *New York Times*. Whether a well-connected media type or just here to

Famous Deli owner David Auspitz wishes you good lox.

eavesdrop, everybody gets the same bad attitude, paper plates and plastic cutlery (700 South 4th Street, 627–9198).

BRUNCH, SEE-AND-BE-SEEN, MANAYUNK: The riverside deck outside the **Manayunk Farmers Market** is a popular pit stop for Sunday bikers, yuppie couples, and all those who appreciate the fun of cruising the excellent food stalls and then finding a place to sit and chow down (4120 Main Street, 483–0100).

BRUNCH BUFFET, 'BURBS: Poached salmon with saffron rice, Lancaster County ham, rare roast beef and an expert omelet set-up at **A.T. Samuels** (Spread Eagle Village, 503 West Lancaster Avenue, Wayne, 610–687–2840).

JAZZ BRUNCH: Philly's most civilized jazz venue, and certainly the best food-wise, **Zanzibar Blue** serves moody gumbos with cool music to ease you into Sunday afternoon (305 South 11th Street, 829–0300).

MINUSCULE RESTAURANT: Tucked away down an alley, so only Chestnut Hillers know where to find the charming and practically microscopic **French Cafe**. Excellent sticky buns and coffee in thick old vintage cups. Lots of baby strollers, too (8624 Germantown Avenue, 247–5959).

SIT-UP-STRAIGHT BRUNCH: **Founders** at the Hotel Atop the Bellevue. The atmosphere's half the attraction, but the food does its part well enough (Broad and Walnut Streets, 893–1776).

SOUL FOOD BRUNCH: Actually, they don't call it brunch at **Mama Rosa's**, the big one in Germantown. But to the famished church-goers who chow down here on some of the best ribs, chicken and macaroni-and-cheese around, it's the gospel according to Sunday breakfast (5531 Germantown Avenue, Mount Airy; 3838 North Broad).

Loaves and Sweets

BAGELS: **Fairmount Bagel Institute's** are bigger and seedier (the poppy and sesame ones, anyway) than most New York bagels, so outrageously plump and firm that they give lox and whitefish the ride of their lives (2501 Olive Street, 235–2245; 267 South 19th Street, 735–2222).

BAKERY, CITY: Reckless sweet-tooth sufferers join the **Painted Parrot Cafe's** dessert club, and have their membership card punched each time they come in for a fudgy brownie or fancy tartlet (209–211 Chestnut Street, 922–5971).

BAKERY, CITY LIMITS: Their best sweet might just be the gooey caramel Ninja bars with chocolate and cashews, but the cheesecakes are pretty super too at **Chase's Original Specialty Bakery** (2135 North 63rd Street, 477–2882).

Don't settle for generic bread! Like fresh-roasted coffees, loaves with integrity and characters all of their own are available throughout Philadelphia and the suburbs.

BAKERY, SOUTH JERSEY: Classic French ways combine with great American desserts like key lime pie and Heath Bar cheesecake at **La Patisserie Francaise**. The espresso ricotta mousse is a sublime pudding for grown-ups. (Kings Highway and Haddon Avenue, Haddonfield, NJ, 609–428–0418).

BAKERY, MANAYUNK: **Main-ly Desserts** shines at Thanksgiving with its justly famous pumpkin pie upholstered in airy pumpkin mousse. You don't need an occasion to enjoy Chocolate Obsession, a lethal pairing of Grand Marnier and chocolate mousses in dark cookie crust (4249 Main Street, Manayunk, 487–1325).

Cups Ahoy:
The Coffeehouse Boom

These days, Philadelphians are sleepless with Seattle-influenced coffee concoctions: foamy cappuccinos, lattes, mochas, jolting espressos and frigid iced caffeine shakes. Here's our short list of the best of what's brewing—a tall order in itself!

COFFEEHOUSE WITH ATTITUDE: Gen-X to the max, **Last Drop Coffeehouse** attracts an unkempt college-age crowd, but welcomes older alternative types, too. Live music on weekends, poetry readings and chess sets for customers with time on their hands (1300 Pine Street, 893–0434).

COFFEE DELICACY: The cappuccino float at **Caribou Cafe**. A tall glass of cappuccino with a luscious scoop of ice cream, at one of the few spots in Center City where you can actually eat after 10 p.m. (1126 Walnut Street, 625–9535).

CUP OF COFFEE, EXPENSIVE: **Ray's Coffee Shop**, the Chinatown coffeeteria that jumpstarted the local java craze, is still a cup

above the rest. The precision brewing process is definitely a show in itself—and the Jamaican Blue Mountain is worth $6 a cup (141 North 9th Street, 922–5122).

GOOD-LOOKING COFFEEHOUSE: **Millennium Coffee's** sleek, contemporary decor features metal chairs that look good but seem designed to prevent prolonged sipping. Diverse crowd, mostly gay. It's

especially pleasant here on sunny days, when the front doors are flung open and tables are set up on the sidewalk (212 South 12th Street, 731–9798).

HIPSTER HANGOUT, CITY: Grunge-style **Quarry Street Cafe** has a sincerely nice staff, comfy couches, a piano, eclectically stocked bookshelves and rocket-fuel java. A post-First Friday must (147 North 3rd Street, 413–1360).

HIPSTER HANGOUT, 'BURBS: Snag a *City Paper*, or snooker your best friend at backgammon at **Cafe Paradiso** in Ardmore. New Harmony Coffees and a tasty, though limited, menu make this the perfect spot to spend a rainy Sunday. Close your eyes and pretend you're in San Francisco (31 East Lancaster Avenue, 610–896–9530).

A knight to remember at Last Drop Coffeehouse.

ICED CAPPUCCINO: Opera Cafe has great coffee (hot and cold), an interesting Italianish menu, sweet service and, best of all, no folk music (1904 Pine Street, 545–3543).

BREAD, SOUTH PHILLY: Some may say it's foolhardy to try and choose, but the firm-crusted loaves from **Cacia's** are so enticing it's hard to get one home without breaking in. Better get two (1218 Mifflin Street, 336–4221).

CONFECTION: Nuts rolled in cocoa and/or caramel and roasted to a crunchy turn distinguish the sophisticated line of sweets from **Society Hill Snacks** in the Manayunk Farmers Market. Don't miss their "mosaic" of fine Valrhona chocolate studded with cashews, walnuts, almonds and dried apricots (4120 Main Street, 483–0100).

Life's one big bread basket for Metropolitan Bakery.

DESSERT, MAIN LINE: Dreamy tollhouse pie at **Marbles**, a lively, casual, high-decibel eatery where everybody who's anybody goes with their small kids in tow (818 Lancaster Avenue, Bryn Mawr, 610–520–9100).

FEATS OF CHOCOLATE: **Aux Petits Delices** in Wayne. There's no end to the chic confections *patissier* Patrick Gauthron can create with chocolate. His wedding cakes are pretty fabulous, too (162 East Lancaster Avenue, Wayne, 610–971–0300).

HANDCRAFTED BREAD, CENTER CITY: **Metropolitan Bakery** creates rustic loaves, baguettes, boules, buns and focaccia with naturally derived "wild" yeasts and herbs. Pick up a few perfect go-withs like goat cheese and fresh baby lettuce (262 South 19th Street, 545–6655; 1114 Pine Street, 627–3433).

HANDCRAFTED BREAD, 'BURBS: **Baker Street** (originally Breadsmith) is Chestnut Hill's morning gathering place and the *only* place in town where the loaves are fragrant and chewy with whole grains and herbs (8009 Germantown Avenue, 248–2500).

HATE-YOURSELF-IN-THE-MORNING DESSERTS: There's sweet consolation from life's worries in the Heath Bar ice cream pie swirled with caramel and myriad other sticky pleasures at **Mick's** (200 South Broad Street, 732–7997; and Willow Grove Mall).

ICE CREAM CAKE: Be brave and try a weird flavor like cinnamon-y Irish Potato, or stick with classic chocolate fudge brownie nut at **Just Ice Cream**, as charming a reproduction of a turn-of-the-century ice cream parlor as ever served a scoop (223 Pennell Road, Aston, 610–497–5550).

ITALIAN BREAD: The round, cross-topped Tuscan loaves at **Sarcone's**, South Philly. Four generations of the family have shaped and shoved them into the same brick oven (758 South 9th Street, 922–0445).

LOW-FAT MUFFINS: **Allspice.** So tasty you'd never guess they contain no nuts, eggs, oil or whole milk (800 South 9th Street, 629–1904)

STICKY BUNS: Regulars wait outside **Rittenhouse Grocers** in the morning for these soft buns big as throw pillows, with *lots* of sticky stuff. So big, in fact, that no one should polish off a whole one by themselves, but . . . (1934 Rittenhouse Square, 732–6000).

SWEET SHOPPE: **Sweet Daddy's**, the Wayne ice creamerie that lures Main Line chocoholics with its intoxicating scents (101 North Wayne Avenue, 610–688–4500).

The Working Lunch

LUNCHTIME ESCAPE FOR IMMATURE ADULTS: Evenings, **Dave & Buster's** may strike anyone over the legal drinking age as a little piece of hell, but try it for a juicy burger in broad daylight at the Bridgeside Grill. With any luck, you'll have the virtual reality game all to yourself (Pier 19 North, 325 N. Delaware Avenue, 413–1951).

CHEAP LUNCH: At **Brigid's**, the Fairmount bar run by ebullient Belgian chef-owner Michel Notredame. For five bucks you get a hearty *plat du jour*, like beef bourguignon over a bed of egg noodles, plus a French roll and salad (726 North 24th Street, 232–3232).

Chef-owner Michel Notredame dishes with diners at Brigid's.

CHEAP CHEAP LUNCH: Roosevelt's Pub, where the half-pound burger-and-fries combo is just $2.95 when you buy a beverage. This extremely basic joint is way better than McDonald's, and McDonald's doesn't serve beer (23rd and Walnut, 557–9722).

OFFICE CATERING: Dean & DeLuca Corporate Catering prepares big, sophisticated sandwiches, and splendid salads with grains and grilled vegetables. Dazzle your meeting mates with desserts from Au Fin Palais and other local bakeries (1601 Market Street, 563–7755; 251 South 18th Street, 893–1420).

CITY LUNCHEONETTE: Early in the morning, when you come in for your egg sandwich and coffee, you'll find the proprietor of Michael's Catering peeling potatoes for lunchtime French fries amid the frenzy of elementary school students clamoring for Tastykakes. Come back at lunchtime for transcendent soft tacos (122 South 22nd Street, 587–9099).

HAND-CARVED TURKEY SANDWICH: The New Corned Beef Academy on Walnut Street. Not as much soul as the original, but plenty of meat (1605 Walnut Street, 561–6222).

INTIMATE LUNCH: Impressive, atmospheric and not all that expensive, in Le Bar Lyonnais, downstairs below Le Bec-Fin. Slip in after the martini-for-lunch crowd has dispersed, take a quiet corner table and call for lentil soup, roast chicken with mashed potatoes or a hearty bistro salad with bacon, potatoes and a poached egg (1523 Walnut Street, 567–1000).

QUICK CIVILIZED LUNCH, CENTER CITY: Cary, a stylish cafe where the burgers are made of yellowfin tuna and the BLT's built on seven-grain black olive bread. Great desserts, too (211 South 15th Street, 735–9100).

QUICK CIVILIZED LUNCH, 'BURBS: Bravo Bistro, darling. But really, what's your hurry? (175 King of Prussia Road, Radnor, 610–293–0161).

Philly Eats:
Our Legendary Junk Foods

For the quintessential Philadelphia meal, begin with a soft pretzel squiggled with mustard and a slice of pizza, progress to a smorgasbord of cheesesteaks and hoagies and follow it up with a cup of water ice. You'd have one heck of a bellyache, but you'd have sampled classic Philly.

Our indigenous urban cuisine, beloved throughout the land, is as legitimate in its own blue-collar way as the jambalayas and po' boys of New Orleans.

A Philly cheesesteak may taste better with provolone, but it's not authentic unless it's oozing that delectable orange "cheese" known simply as "Whiz."

Decades of sampling such low-brow foods have given us a unique perspective: no matter how good a South Philly sub might be, a territorial Great Northeasterner would insist that *his* local hoagerie made a better product. There'd be no compromise, so, in the interest of fairness and equal time, we present a spicy, greasy, utterly delicious compendium of our all-time Philly phood phavorites.

CHEESESTEAK, CENTER CITY: **Jim's Steaks**. Meaty, cheesy, salty and fragrantly familiar: the classic 3 a.m. steak, complete with a sidewalk sideshow that's never the same and always amusing (400 South Street, 928–1911).

CHEESESTEAK, PERENNIAL: In 1990, we enlisted nationally renowned *Roadfood* authors and gastronomes Jane and Michael Stern to help us choose Philly's finest. After sampling nine hoagies, the duo selected **Mama's**, an unassuming shop where they pile the beef inside the roll. Years later, the quality's still high (426 Belmont Avenue, Bala Cynwyd, 610–664–4757).

CHEESESTEAK, MAIN LINE: Not too big but extremely potent, the two-fisted hunger-buster comes hot off the grill at **Mallory's Restaurant** (863 Lancaster Avenue, Bryn Mawr, 610–527–5870).

CHEESESTEAK, SOUTH JERSEY: They drive over from Cherry Hill because **Gatano's** does a masterful job with its drippy, no-nonsense sandwich. It's the onions (205 South White Horse Pike, Stratford, 609–783–1177).

EARLY MORNING TREAT: Drive to the **Federal Pretzel Bakery** before 11 a.m. for soft pretzels—fresh, warm and cheap, right out of the oven (638 Federal Street, 467–0505).

HOAGIE, CITY: **Salumeria**, for the garlicky Caesar dressing they brush heavily on the roll, for delectable extras like chopped artichoke hearts, and for the way it ages so deliciously in your refrigerator so that *tomorrow*, it's even better than today (Reading Terminal Market; The Market at 30th Street Station).

HOAGIE ALTERNATIVE: The Vietnamese hoagie at **Cafe Phuong** in the Chinatown Mall combines liver pâté, Vietnamese chicken roll, pastrami, thinly shaved cucumbers, parsley, hot peppers, pickled carrots and radishes in a French roll—a great culinary argument for the melting pot (11th and Race Streets, no phone).

HOAGIE DELIVERY: **Marie's Variety** in South Philly, open every night until 11 p.m. The prosciutto with provolone and Genoa salami is a taste of Italy brought to your door (1311 West Moyamensing Avenue, 336–8882).

HOAGIE, MAIN LINE: Tozzi's, affiliated with the renowned Jersey shore sandwich shop Dino's of Margate, is a relative sophisticate in the hoagie field (383 West Lancaster Avenue, Wayne, 610–964–9007).

HOAGIE, NORTHEAST: At Slack's Hoagie Shack, they're dressed to kill in spicy vinaigrette, with dainty slivers of onion and a shower of angel's-hair lettuce (2499 Aramingo Avenue, 423–4020; 8445 Frankford Avenue, 338–6777).

HOAGIE, SOUTH JERSEY: Carmen's Cold Cuts offers a neatly constructed packet of meats and cheeses, snuggled into a firm torpedo roll (42 East Browning Road, Bellmawr, 609–931–7203).

Geno's cheese-steaks are good to the last bite.

HOAGIE, SOUTH PHILLY: Imagine our surprise when we learned that Geno's, the vaunted cheesesteakerie, produces an inspired cold hoagie! It's spicy, sloppy, stand-up fare at the most famous sandwich corner in the city—longtime rival Pat's is right across the street (1219 South 9th Street at Passyunk Avenue, 389–1455).

HOAGIE, UP-AND-COMER: Rocco's Italian special at DiGulielmo's takes top honors. Their sandwich of crisp, freshly breaded chicken with mustard mayonnaise, a trend in the making, is equally ambrosial (Reading Terminal Market; Downstairs in the Bellevue, Broad and Walnut Streets).

HOT DOG, CITY: Franks A-Lot has a winner of a weiner. These plump links really stand out, and the chili's grand (Reading Terminal Market, 12th and Filbert Streets, 625–9991).

HOT DOG, MAIN LINE: Regular dogs, jumbo dogs, turkey dogs, jalapeno dogs, all-beef dogs, cheese dogs and Polish sausage—all grilled and doused with your choice of notably fresh toppings or tangy Texas weiner sauce at cheerful new

Ardmore hot doggerie **Herbie's**. This guy is *serious* about his pups (12 West Lancaster Avenue, 610–642–1414).

MILKSHAKE, CITY: With just a smidge of grown-up alcohol, the Chocolate Monkey at **TGI Friday's** (500 South 2nd Street, 625–8389; 18th Street and the Benjamin Franklin Parkway, 665–8443; also in Bensalem, King of Prussia and Bala Cynwyd).

MILKSHAKE, 'BURBS: The stellar chocolate shake at **Wynnewood Pharmacy**, an enormously well-stocked drugstore that seems to carry every perfume ever made, and then some (Wynnewood Road, Wynnewood, 610–642–9091).

MILKSHAKE, SOUTH PHILLY: At pink-collar **Millie's Luncheonette**, hon. And mind your manners—everybody in the place knows that you're not from the neighborhood (1441 Shunk Street, 467–8553).

"out of this world!"

TASTYKAKE

A 1940's Tastykake ad pays tribute to the timeless Philly treat.

NOSTALGIC DESSERT: True Philadelphians brook no criticism of **Tastykake**—they eat it for breakfast, no apologies. Baked in the Nicetown neighborhood of the Northeast at a rate of 2.5 million boxes a week, the 71 varieties of cakes and pies provide sugar-high snacks for millions who wouldn't have it any other way. Krimpets, of course, are klassic.

PIZZA: Pizza is so beloved in Philly that the whole concept is tied to our heartstrings with long tendrils of gooey mozzarella. But it's worth the trip to the Great Northeast, where **Cafe Michelangelo** seems too Italian to be real: boccie courts, authentic *rustica* fare and charming proprietors (11901 Bustleton Avenue, 698–2233).

PIZZA, CENTER CITY: **Savas** dishes up a great basic pie. Each ingredient asserts itself without ever suffocating the others—although the alligator topping *is* a bit much. Stick with sausage (1547 Spring Garden Street, 564–1920).

Harking back to the 1820s, the soft pretzel, a classic sidewalk snack, is a long-standing and delicious Philadelphia tradition.

PIZZA, MAIN LINE: The "abbondanza"—i.e., the works—pie at **Boccie** is so much more delicious here than at less upscale parlors. Each humble ingredient holds its own deliciously (Suburban Square, 104 Coulter Avenue, Ardmore, 610–658–0580).

PIZZA, ROMANTIC: At **Marra's**, a proud old family restaurant in the heart of the "downtown" South Philly shopping zone, you can hide away in the big dark wooden booths, alone with one of the best bar pies in town. The sauce is extra spicy (1734 East Passyunk Avenue, 463–9249).

PIZZA, SOUTH JERSEY: **Arianna's** crowns its thin, crisp crusts with sizzling goat cheese, prosciutto and sundried tomatoes (The Marketplace, 1990 Route 70 East, Cherry Hill, NJ, 609–751–2002).

A platter of pretzels hot from the oven at Fisher's Pretzel Stand.

PIZZA, WHITE: Since its first Best of Philly™ recognition, this tiny pizza joint in Port Richmond has upgraded to become a *big* pizza joint. But **Tacconelli's** still has its original brick oven, and they still make you call to reserve dough for your pie so they don't run out in the time it takes you to drive there (2604 East Somerset Street, 425–4983).

PRETZEL, PERENNIAL: As long as the friendly Mennonites at **Fisher's** keep dipping the freshly baked twists in melted

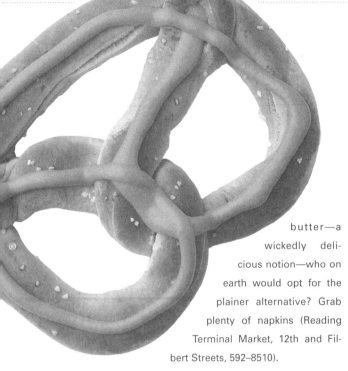

butter—a wickedly delicious notion—who on earth would opt for the plainer alternative? Grab plenty of napkins (Reading Terminal Market, 12th and Filbert Streets, 592–8510).

| The soft pretzel with mustard, a Philly classic.

PRETZEL CONTENDER: Les' Pretzels are gigantic and ropy, with delicate crusts and insides as densely satisfying as nougat. Find them at You Bet Your Sweet Ice (2442 Cottman Avenue).

PRETZEL LORE: For those hooked on the salty curves of the Philly soft pretzel, a visit to the **Pretzco Inc. Soft Pretzel Bakery & Museum** is in order. Tucked away in a shopping center, it's not the most impressive of museums, but you won't come away hungry (Riverview Plaza, Delaware Avenue, 463–1880).

PRETZEL TWIST: Chocolate-dipped and encrusted with buttery toffee crackle at **Zitner's** North 17th Street headquarters, and sold at confectionery shops around the city (229–4990).

ROAST PORK SANDWICH: For South Philly's version of the power lunch, line up on the sidewalk with cops, construction workers and wide-lapel attorneys for savory pork with aged sharp provolone, *broccoli di rape* and plenty of atmosphere at venerable **Tony Luke's** (39 East Oregon Avenue, 551–5725).

VEGETARIAN HOAGIE: Chickie's Italian Deli—baked eggplant, roasted peppers, broccoli rabe and sharp provolone on bread from Sarcone's. With flavors like this, who needs salami? (1014 Federal Street, 462–8040).

WATER ICE: A three-way tie between South Philly's top contenders, all of whom scoop up a superlative blend of ice and slush and summer-sidewalk atmosphere: **Pop's** (1337 Oregon Avenue), **Italiano's** (12th and Shunk Streets) and **Joe's Homemade Water Ice** (1514 Snyder Avenue). Phone numbers are not included because water ice is a seasonal thing, and you don't *call* first—you just show up!

WATER ICE, SOUTH JERSEY: Lite-n-Up, the tartest and slushiest (603 Station Avenue, Haddon Heights, NJ).

WATER ICE, NORTHEAST: Nick's in Mayfair is run by a retired city cop who has now dedicated himself to this sweet seasonal pursuit (Cottman and Montague Avenues, 333–6005).

Asian Delights

CHINESE FOOD DELIVERY, CENTER CITY: Open late for takeout, eat-in or transportation to your doorstep, **Noodle Heaven** on Broad Street. For those roast pork cravings that just won't quit (220–224 Broad Street, 735–6191).

CHINESE RESTAURANT: The reserved Taiwanese chef **Susanna Foo** presides over one of the best Chinese restaurants in the *country*, with a menu that marries East and West in the most felicitous way. It's *certainly* the best Chinese restaurant in town. Transcendent dim sum leads the way to suave permutations of Eastern ingredients and classic techniques. Decor is

dark and plain, with lots of mirrors—a restrained backdrop for outstanding food (1512 Walnut Street, 545–2666).

CHINATOWN RESTAURANT, QUIET: **Golden Pond**, as tranquil as its name would indicate, especially amid the urban clangor of China-

> The best Chinese food in town is at Susanna Foo.

town's streets. Try the yin-yang soup (1006 Race Street, 923–0303).

CHINATOWN RESTAURANT, NOISY: Savvy eaters from the neighborhood and beyond have discovered **Tai Lake**, a cavernous Hong Kong-style establishment. Part of the excitement is due to those tanks full of live fish, ensuring the freshest seafood possible. Steamed whole sea bass is a must (134 North 10th Street, 922–0698).

CHINESE RESTAURANT THAT FEELS LIKE HONG KONG: **Ocean Harbor**, the loud, king-sized eatery with stellar dim sum and swimmingly fresh fish (1023 Race Street, 547–1398).

CHINATOWN RESTAURANT, VEGETARIAN: The trend in Chinatown is toward "natural healthy cuisine," featuring *trompe l'oeoil* "meats" deliciously crafted from wheat or soy. The most promising contender thus far is **Charles Plaza** (234–236 North 10th Street, 829–4283).

CHINESE RESTAURANT PATRONIZED BY PEOPLE FROM THE NEIGHBORHOOD: Relentlessly unglamorous, with blistering bright lights and exemplary Cantonese home cooking, **Shiao Lan Kung** (930 Race Street, no phone).

CHINESE RESTAURANT, NOT IN CHINATOWN: Modest and engaging, an oasis off South Street, **Mustard Greens** cuts the mustard with style and no MSG. A dish of healthy greens is always on the menu (622 South 2nd Street, 627–0833).

CHINESE RESTAURANT, SLEEPER: A few savvy Philadelphians know that way out on Lancaster Avenue, in a restaurant alongside a Dairy Queen, the brother of Susanna Foo presents exquisite renditions of classic dishes, brightened with the freshest vegetables at **Silk Road** (414 Lancaster Avenue, Devon, 610–963–7625).

CHINESE RESTAURANT, 'BURBS: Yangming is a favorite with Main Liners craving dumplings, seafood and basic Sunday-night Chinese fare in a highly efficient atmosphere. They do things with tomatoes at this big, glitzy spot that you've never *seen* in a Chinese restaurant. Cooking classes and wine seminars are also offered (1051 Conestoga Road, Bryn Mawr, 610–527–3200).

> # Drive along Race or Arch Streets and Chinatown may not look like much. In order to truly savor its scents, sounds and flavors, park the car and explore on foot.

DIM SUM, CHINATOWN: The dumplings come thick and fast at **Tsui Hung Chung**, and you can usually get a straight answer about any mysterious-looking morsel from the bamboo steamer before venturing a taste. Night-owl alert: it's open until 2 a.m.! (911–913 Race Street, 925–8901).

HOT AND SOUR SOUP: Made without meat at **Harmony Chinese Vegetarian**, so full-bodied and delicious, the only giveaway is the clear, grease-free surface (135 North 9th Street, 627–4520).

INDIAN RESTAURANT, HUMBLE: Vindaloonies have their choice of several all-you-can-eat buffets near the Penn campus, but **Tandoor India**'s is the right combination of cheap and stimulating. The sitdown menu also curries favor (106 South 40th Street, 222–7122).

The entrance to Chinatown— a gateway to great food.

INDIAN RESTAURANT, GRAND: Don't be put off by **Palace of Asia's** surprising location inside a Ramada Inn at the Fort Washington exit of the Turnpike. At this opulent dining parlor, the vindaloos are properly searing, the raitas cool and the spices a swirl of exotic flavors. One of the area's most beautiful restaurants (285 Commercial Drive, 646–2133).

PEKING DUCK: Mai Lai Wah, known for noodles, also serves a luscious bird of a differnt feather (1001 Race Street, 627-2610).

PLACE TO TAKE A GINGER ADDICT: The gracious women who run **Rangoon,** the city's only Burmese restaurant, make a salad in which fresh, julienned ginger is the primary ingredient; crunchy dried chickpeas, tomatoes and sesame seeds also dance in delicious attendance (145 North 9th Street, 829–8939).

THAI RESTAURANT, CITY: The room may not be much to look at, but the food's knowingly herbed and spiced at **Lemon Grass.** Definitely try the sticky rice, basil salmon and ugly duckling (3626 Lancaster Avenue, 222–8042).

THAI RESTAURANT, 'BURBS: With its blistering curries and mild pad thai noodles, **Thai Pepper** is the Main Line's favorite Thai break (64 East Lancaster Avenue, Ardmore, 610–629–9939).

VIETNAMESE RESTAURANT: Since South Philly's Asian population far exceeds that of Chinatown, it's no surprise that **Vinh Hoa** is a stone's throw from the Italian Market. Lush sheaves of fresh basil and other herbs are just waiting to get themselves into fragrant dishes (746 Christian Street, 925–0307).

Italian Accents

CASUAL MEAL: Primavera, for silken pastas, amusing specials and salads concocted by someone who cares—then drizzled with olive oil pressed by the chef's father in Italy (146 South Street, 925–7832; 384 West Lancaster Avenue, Wayne, 610–254–0200).

ITALIAN RESTAURANT, 'BURBS: The food at **Toscana Cucina Rustica** is so lustily Tuscan, garlic-laced beans, great grilled meats, antipasto anointed with hot-pepper olive oil—it's hard to believe you're on a Main Line side street (24 North Merion Avenue, Bryn Mawr, 610–527–7700).

ITALIAN RESTAURANT, GREAT NORTHEAST: Isabella is an outpost of sophisticated charm and old-world civility in its blue-collar neighborhood. Do try the *tagliatelle alla Siciliana*, swimming with julienned eggplant, and save room for the ricotta cheesecake (6516 Castor Avenue, 533–0356).

> **Primavera Pizza in Ardmore, a relative of Primavera, is also ideal for a cheery, casual meal.**

ITALIAN FOOD BEFORE THE THEATER: Succumb to the fey pizzas at **Upstares at Varalli**—perhaps one smeared with arugula pesto and festooned with grilled shrimp—and follow it up with a savory main-course risotto (1345 Locust Street, 546–4200).

OLIVE TREATMENT: Breaded, fried and stuffed with sausage at **Tutto Misto** (603 South 3rd Street, 627–2803).

LASAGNA: At **Jimmy's Milan**, it's packed with meats, cheeses and spices, with enough left over for tomorrow's breakfast (okay, we *really* like lasagna) (39 South 19th Street, 563–2499).

OSSO BUCO TO GO: When you want Italian at home, beyond the usual takeout lasagna and veal parmesan, pull over at **Rago's** in Lafayette Hill (517 Germantown Pike, 610–834–5557).

RESTAURANT THAT'S ALSO A STORE: Bring wine, grab a couple of seats in the crowded dining area and settle in to savor huge portions of delicious homemade pasta and salads at **Grecco's Italian Market & Cafe.** Pick up provolone, olive oil and other comestibles when you pay the check (321 Lancaster Avenue, Exton, 610–594–9909).

South Philly:
The Italian Market and More

It was in this working-class area south of South Street and north of Veterans Stadium that Sylvester Stallone's Rocky lived, sparred and slugged those sides of beef. The best way to experience South Philly's enclave of Italian-American culture is to eat until your waistband demands unbuttoning, but only after shopping at the old-fashioned street vendors' stands along Ninth Street, in the gritty soul of the Italian Market.

You name it, you can probably find it among the myriad of stores and vendors in the Italian Market.

BISCOTTI: For twice-baked cookies to dip in a cup of inky espresso or gnaw savagely when the world gets under your skin, visit the grand *pasticceria* **A. Nichol's Italian Pastries** (2550 South 3rd Street, 755–2460).

CASUAL DINNER: Felicia's is lively with diners digging into light, crispy fried calamari, succulent lasagna and savory radicchio salads (1148 South 11th Street, 755–9656).

DOSE OF GARLIC: South Philly's most stylish restaurant, with its blue neon and reggae in the background, is also its most garlic-conscious. You get a whole head of roasted cloves with your bread at **Aglio**—best followed up with a bowl of the velvety, mellow garlic soup (937 East Passyunk Avenue, 336–8008).

ITALIAN SAUSAGE: Sonny D'Angelo on 9th Street also makes amazing *boudin* and other worldly links, but until you've grilled his pork-mozzarella-fresh basil sausage in your own backyard, you simply haven't lived (909 South 9th Street, 923–5637).

OLIVE OIL: Claudio's, Italian Market. Unless you're not from the neighborhood and can't grin and bear the salesclerks' teasing (924 South 9th Street, 627–1873).

OLIVE SALAD: DiBruno Brothers, an old-fashioned grocery store in the Italian Market, packs on the garlic and oregano when preparing this lusty Italian condiment, so right on a salami hoagie (930 South 9th Street, 922–2876).

PLACE TO GET MOONSTRUCK: Roselena's Coffee Bar, a romantic little cafe decorated with old wedding portraits of South Philly couples. Try the dessert perfected by Michelangelo's mother. Yes, *that* Michelangelo (1623 East Passyunk Avenue, 755–9697).

PLACE TO GO BEFORE A DAYTIME GAME AT THE VET: Medora's Mecca has cheap-and-cheerful pasta in deep bowls, and meatball hoagies guaranteed to drip on your shoes (3101 South 13th Street, 336–1655).

PLACES TO GO BEFORE OR AFTER A NIGHT GAME AT THE VET: Philadium Tavern for spaghetti and clams (1631 Packer Avenue, 339–8232), or Marra's Restaurant for pizza bubbly with cheese (1734 East Passyunk Avenue, 463–9249).

PROSCIUTTO: The genuine article, hog heaven for lovers of this extra-special imported Italian ham, at Cilione's (1726 Jackson Street, 389–4255).

SOUVENIR: A cookie tin from Termini Bros. bakery, the classic South Philly calling card for funerals, holidays and other occasions since 1921.

Philadelphians have long been sweet on Termini Bros.

Inside, find old-fashioned Jordan almonds, delectable *scumetti* crunchy with crushed almonds and cashews and myriad other traditional Italian sweets (1523 South 8th Street, 1–800–882–7650).

CHRISTMAS EVE DINNER: In this neighborhood, the

traditional December 24th repast consists of "seven fishes," and involves slaving over a hot stove for hours. Or you could tuck your napkin under your chin at **Dante & Luigi's** and work your way through *baccala* (codfish) in red or white sauce, fried smelts and five other swimmingly good courses (762 South 10th Street, 922–9501).

NEIGHBORHOOD RESTAURANT: Dom DeLuise's favorite, and no wonder: **Frankie's Seafood Italiano** is an old-school joint where the portions are huge, the atmosphere is convivial and the succulent clams on your linguine are always pristinely fresh (1100 Tasker Street, 468–9989).

PLACE TO OVEREAT: Locals put on the feedbag at **Joseph's Italian Cuisine**, where the eponymous young chef loads his pasta creations with crabmeat, asparagus, rich sauces and other irresistibles (1915 East Passyunk Avenue, 755–2770).

RESTAURANT IN SOUTH PHILLY: And, arguably, in the entire city: the vaguely anachronistic, dignified **Saloon**. A burnished parlor of antiquities, serving top-notch Italian and Continental food. Every big shot in town eats here—join them (750 South 7th Street, 627–1811).

SOUTH PHILLY SLEEPER: **Mr. Martino's Trattoria**, a modest, engaging polenta-and-*salsiccia* joint in a former hardware store that was a former stable. Sitting here, it feels like a hundred years ago, except for Sinatra crooning from the tape deck (1646 East Passyunk Avenue, 755–0663).

Down-Home Delicious

BARBECUED BRISKET: When it's cooked long and slow the way they do it at **Phoebe's Bar B-Q**, the tender shreds melt in your mouth (2214 South Street, 546–4811).

BORSCHT: Hot or cold, it's imperial scarlet ambrosia at **Warsaw Cafe** (306 South 16th Street, 435–0204).

COMFORT FOOD, DINNER: June Cleaver is everybody's mom at **Momi**, where the Tater Tots and Tang are just the way you remember them, but the meat loaf's a whole lot better (526 South 4th Street, 625–0310).

DINER: Judge for yourself whether the legendary butter cookies deserve all the ballyhoo at **Melrose Diner**, but those classic, long-suffering waitresses, those stainless-steel fixtures, and that weird midnight *zeitgeist* make this, undeniably, a true-blue American diner (1501 Snyder Avenue, 467–6644).

DINER, NORTHEAST PHILLY: The *best* brisket—juicy and stringy, the way it's supposed to be—plus lovingly mashed potatoes and soulful gravy at **Country Club Restaurant & Pastry Shop**, the Northeast diner that grew up, tied on an apron and *really* started cooking (1717 Cottman Avenue, 722–0500).

DINER, RETRO: Lime rickeys, chicken à la king, patty melts like you remember them and shiny red booths to chow down in, at the authentic **American Diner.** Come dessert-time, the chocolate bread pudding is a deep, dark must-have (435 Spring Garden Street, 592–8838, 4201 Chestnut Street, 387–1451).

FRIED CHICKEN: Savor some of the best, along with plenty of other toothsome home cooking, at **Salaam**, owned by music producer and Motown songwriter Kenny Gamble, of Gamble and Huff/Philadelphia International fame (1501 Christian Street, 731–1590).

JEWISH HOME COOKING: Stuffed cabbage, blintzes, kugels and cinnamon rolls at **Irene's Kitchen**. Next time you're sick, stop in for a quart of her highly effective, over-the-counter chicken soup (133 South 20th Street, 567–3249).

MUSSELS: The classic South Philly shellfish presentation, in a classic South Philly restaurant, steamed with plenty of garlic and piled high for finger-licking consumption, is at its cheap-and-cheerful best at humble **Triangle Tavern** (10th and Reed Streets, 467–8683).

PEACH COBBLER: For sweet dessert after transcendent barbecued ribs or Cajun curried chicken, try **Lip Licn's II** (4909 Catharine Street, 471–5477)

PULLED-PORK BARBECUE: Shredded, juicy pork with North Carolina-style vinegar sauce is a whiff of Southern comfort on a soft, seeded bun from the **Down Home Diner**, a chowhound's classic dive revisited, and a gem among Reading Terminal Market's myriad eateries (12th and Filbert Streets, 627–1955).

SMOKED TURKEY: At the deliciously scented **Smokin' Sam's Italian Grill.** Sample the smoked duck, as well. And the smoked brisket. And the smoked fish. . . (417 Germantown Avenue, Lafayette Hill, 941–4652).

Seafood Divine

LOBSTER: No ifs, ands or butter substitutes, just properly steamed three-pounders served with respect at that first-rate steakhouse, the **Palm** (200 South Broad Street, 546–PALM).

FISH RESTAURANT, HUMBLE: The freshest swimmers appear on your table at **BLT's Cobblefish,** a funky BYO cafe in a working-class neighborhood, with an utterly sophisticated attitude toward food (443 Shurs Lane, Manayunk, 483–5478).

FISH RESTAURANT, GRAND: Impress yourself and your guests at **Striped Bass,** the pricey, high-profile palace of seafood in a grand old Art Deco space that's revitalized the Center City dining scene. An oceanful of tasty vernaculars, from grilled shrimp tamales to skate ribs with wakame seaweed (1500 Walnut Street, 732–4444).

> **Haute decor and dishes are the bait at Striped Bass.**

HARDSHELL CRABS: Skip the gooky chowder and proceed directly to the garlic crabs at unpretentious **Benny the Bum's,** beloved in the Great Northeast and deserving of a wider audience (9991 Bustleton Avenue, 673–3000).

OYSTERS: David Mink, proprietor of **Sansom Street Oyster House** is a fanatic for freshness, and knows the provenance of every piece of shellfish he serves up steamed, fried or on the half-shell. This plain, old-Philly establishment is worth a visit for its convivial bar and dining room festooned with antique majolica oyster plates (1516 Sansom Street, 567–7683).

PRESENTATION OF SMOKED SALMON: Michel's salmon napoleon is a great wall of rosy leaves, stacked high and "cemented" with airy salmon mousse at this French-via-California import (Latham Hotel, 17th and Walnut Streets, 563–9444).

SALMON: Cutters Grand Cafe has Pacific king salmon, grilled on mesquite coals and drizzled with lemon-vermouth butter as subtle as a French kiss (2005 Market Street, 851–6262).

SOFT-SHELLED CRABS: The ones at Alisa Cafe grab you and hold you tight. So do lots of other dishes at this lovely little *boite* near the 69th Street Terminal, a stalwart survivor from the mid-70's Philadelphia Restaurant Renaissance (109 Fairfield Avenue, Upper Darby, 610–352–4402).

SUSHI, CENTER CITY: Intimate and inviting, Genji II (an "import" from University City) takes its sashimi and hand rolls seriously (1720 Sansom Street, 564–1720).

SUSHI, ELSEWHERE: Serene, two-story Hikaru—finally, the essential restaurant Manayunk deserves, complete with tatami room and sardonic chefs. Ask for a window seat (4838 Main Street, 487–3500).

> **A school of aesthetic and appetizing dishes can be found at Hikaru.**

SUSHI SPECTACLE: The gleaming stainless-steel "robot" produces pristine cakes of garnished rice and rolls at Fuji Mountain (2030 Chestnut Street, 751–0939).

Haute Stuff

RESTAURANT: The **Fountain** at the Four Seasons, with something for everyone in the grand hotel tradition. Even if you've never toured the sparkling kitchens downstairs, or been invited to the coveted chef's dinner in the kitchen, one meal is enough to forge a commitment (1 Logan Square, 18th and Cherry Streets, 963–1500).

PLACE TO TALK ABOUT WHAT YOU'RE EATING: The venerable **La Truffe** has hopped on the "chef's table" bandwagon. Co-owners Les Smith and Jeannine Mermet take turns hosting the monthly dinners and explaining the "sensory elements" of every menu decision (10 South Front Street, 925–5062).

FRENCH FOOD, BUCKS COUNTY: In an ancient stone farmhouse on a hill above riff-raffish New Hope, **La Bonne Auberge** remains a gracious outpost of grand French food. Ever so slightly stuffy, but worth the hauteur (Village II, Mechanic Street, New Hope, 862–2462).

FRENCH FOOD, CITY: Actually, the best in the entire *country* is found at **Le Bec-Fin**, if you agree with the innumerable food critics bowled over by irrepressible Lyonnais chef Georges Perrier and the exacting service, atmosphere and food at his rococo dining parlor. Not for the faint of pocketbook (1523 Walnut Street, 567–1000).

The man behind Le Bec-Fin, chef-owner Georges Perrier.

It takes a steady hand... A delicious detail is added to one of many desserts at Le Bec-Fin.

FRENCH FOOD, SOUTH JERSEY: The only thing that would make gracious **La Campagne** better is a liquor license. On the other hand, the lack thereof helps keep the prices down at this suburban French country inn, expertly cheffed by Olivier de Saint-Martin (312 Kresson Road, Cherry Hill, 609–429–7647).

Chef-owner Jean-Francois Taquet offers fine food and decor at his namesake Taquet.

FRENCH FOOD, SUBURBS: Taquet, namesake of Jean-Francois Taquet, a talented young *maitre cuisinier de France* who presents a stunning combination of grand know-how and casual, bistro-esque food (The Wayne Hotel, 139 East Lancaster Avenue, Wayne, 610–296–2131).

GHOST: The Hessian soldier at the **General Wayne Inn**. According to legend, he was buried alive within the cellar walls. A former manager saw him whip a dinner roll across the room. All we want to know is, can he make it to the Best of Philly™ party? (625 Montgomery Avenue, Merion, 610–664–5125).

PLACE TO HOLD A PRIVATE PARTY: Every detail is attended to **Passerelle**, including the most lavish flower arrangements on the Main Line (175 King of Prussia Road, Radnor, 293–9411).

ELEGANT SURROUNDINGS: If you want to seduce someone with sheer grandeur, whisk them off to **Ciboulette**, inside the Bellevue. At this topnotch restaurant, serving the regional tastes of France in small, chic portions, such vestiges of the venerable hotel's architectural magnificence as fat marble pillars and carved plaster ceilings make the setting nothing short of breathtaking (200 South Broad Street, 790–1210).

UNDER-RECOGNIZED RESTAURANT: Chanterelles, the petite parlor on Spruce Street in the space that housed Le Bec-Fin back in its humble old days. Gifted young chef Philippe Chin is creating some of the classiest French-inspired *prix fixes* in Center City, for pretheater dining or leisurely indulgence (1312 Spruce Street, 735–7110).

Wine Tuning

BIGGEST WINE LIST: Compiled in a bound book as big as a half case of Brunello di Montalcino, the largely Italian collection at **La Famiglia Ristorante**—11,000 bottles—outweighs any wine list in the city. Pinch pennies with a $20 Chianti, or sip a top-shelf $300 Amarone (8 South Front Street, 922–2803).

WAY FOR OENOPHILES TO MAKE IT THROUGH THE WINTER: Swirl, sniff and sip at the annual Philadelphia Wine Festival held at the **Ritz-Carlton**. From January through April, winemakers from first-rate producers around the world host dinners and tastings (Liberty Place at 17th and Chestnut Streets, 563–1600).

WINE CHAT: Unpretentious British "wine-osaur" **Phillip Silverstone**, co-host of "Time Out For Fine Wine" on WFLN. He does his best to "de-stuffify" wines, gets headaches at tastings and considers himself more of an anecdotist than an expert.

WINES BY THE GLASS: Sip your way through a flight of white Bordeaux at the bar, or accompany a plateful of delicious ravioli with sample after sample of domestic bubbly at **Ristorante Panorama**, a first-rate Italian brasserie convenient to Old City and the historic district (14 North Front Street at Market Street, 922–7800).

WINE TASTINGS, ADVANCED: Since the **Independent Wine Club** hosts approximately 60 oeno-happenings a year, chances are there's an appealing one right around the corner. Under the direction of the affable, unpretentious Neal Ewing, all tastings are held in the dim, clubby private room upstairs at Jack's Firehouse (2130 Fairmount Avenue; call 610–649–9936 for information).

WINE STORE, SOUTH JERSEY: It's worth a trek to downtown Camden to shop in the "Camden Catacombs" wine cellar at **Triangle Liquors**. Owner Dave Moore runs a sophisticated wine department dedicated to bringing the best from small producers all over the world. This is the place to buy Le Bec-Fin's house wine, Ampeau Cote de Beaune Village—and incidentally, Moore is the brother of Le Bec-Fin's sommelier, Greg Moore (1200 Broadway at Kaighns Avenue, Camden, 609–365–1800).

WINE STORE, CITY: The state's costliest State Store, the **Wine Reserve** is also one of the few that keep bottles properly horizontal, instead of standing them upright to save on space. More than 800 wines from a dozen countries, and not a liter of plonk in sight. This place brought State Stores into the 20th century (205 South 18th Street, 560–4529).

WINE STORE, MAIN LINE: The one in **Narberth** next to the train station. Cool salesguys, big and roomy, with a very un-Liquor-Control-Board-like back room where the good stuff is stashed (1 Station Circle, 610–664–4699).

Meat and Potatoes:
Philly's Great Steaks

Rib-eye or T-bone? Whichever cut you prefer, you can get a heroically good steak at any of the following establishments. Each presents a slightly different spin on the traditional steakhouse and the "extras"—lobster, salads, potato side dishes galore.

ATMOSPHERE: **Ruth's Chris** has a pleasant air of faded gentility, and big, romantic booths for snuggling and sharing a thick steak. Beware, fine dressers: the glorious steaks sizzle so violently with butter on their scalding-hot metal platters, you *must* shield your finery with lots of napkins (260 South Broad Street, 790–1515).

BUTCHER: **Heebner's Meats** at the Lancaster Farmers Market. Shapely ribs, gorgeous roasts and friendly, robust meat-cutters (Route 30 and Eagle Road, Strafford, 610–687–0307).

CAESAR SALAD: Tucked away on a side street, **Morton's of Chicago** is a dim haven of blessed anonymity. The waiters, who act as if they were born in the place, flourish the raw meats before you to help you decide. Side dishes lack pizzazz, but the tossed-at-table Caesar salad makes a perfect platemate for the big prime steaks (1 Logan Square between 19th and Cherry Streets, 557–0724).

PARTY FOOD: **Ham Sweet Ham** is a popular favorite, where it's spiral sliced, honey glazed and better than baked ham has a right to be (Gwynedd Crossing Shopping Center, Routes 309 and 63, North Wales, 654–9400).

PORTION: The **Saloon** isn't exactly a steakhouse, but this swell South Philly establishment has an artfully clubby ambiance and an air of quiet timelessness—*and* a 20-ounce sirloin that's nothing short of transcendent (750 South 7th Street, 627–1811).

Started in 1969 as a neighborhood bar and spaghetti joint, the Saloon now serves one of the city's finest steaks.

The walls have ears, and eyes, and noses....Celebrity caricatures oversee the lively scene at the Palm.

SERVICE: Perhaps the highest praise for the **Palm** is that nobodies and out-of-towners are treated with the same quiet deference accorded the important (and self-important) Philadelphians whose painted likenesses grace the portrait-crammed walls (200 South Broad Street, 546–7256).

SIDE DISHES: Creamed spinach like Mom never made it, too rich for words. Lyonnais potatoes speckled with bits of irresistibly crunchy onion. Big scarlet slabs of tomato interleaved with snowy mozzarella. All this and more at **Kansas City Prime**, Manayunk's modish, pricey steakhouse (4417 Main Street, 482–3700).

And Yet More Great Food!

CALIFORNIA-STYLE FOOD: **Michel's**, an offshoot of LA's chi-chi Citrus, is a bright setting for Center City dining. Unique revisions of classic foods (hope you like your tuna sandwich almost raw!), lush salads and lovely desserts are on the menu, along with a Cali-centric wine list (Latham Hotel, 17th and Walnut Streets, 563–9444).

CHEESE DIP: **Viennese Cafe**, Cherry Hill. With seven, count 'em, *seven* cheeses. Served as an appetizer, or by the pound, to go (1442 Route 70 East, 609–795–0172).

EXPERIMENTAL COOKING: *And* service, *and* sommeliers: at the **Restaurant School**, the institution that has spawned hundreds of chefs in Philly and beyond (4207 Walnut Street, 222–2400).

40-COURSE MEAL: The Middle Eastern *mezze* spread at **Cedar's Restaurant**. Those plates just keep on coming, so don't fill up on hummus, grape leaves and falafel (616 South 2nd Street, 925–4950).

FRENCH FRIES: Waffled in a mouth-pleasing, criss-cross cut, perfectly seasoned and just a *little* bit spicy, at **Carolina's Restaurant & Bar** (333 Belrose Lane, Radnor, 610–293–1000).

GOOD-LOOKING RESTAURANT: A big slice of sophistication in a blue-collar neighborhood of the Great Northeast, **Napoleon Cafe** is a series of painterly rooms where you're served simple pastas and exquisite desserts (2652 East Somerset Street, 739–6979).

> Works of art, even painterly porcines, find a comfortable atmosphere at Napoleon Cafe.

GUACAMOLE: No matter which delectable enchilada or Mexican platter you try at **12th Street Cantina** in Reading Terminal (or its sister, **Cantina on Main** in the Manayunk Farmers Market), it goes better with a side order of buttery, spicy mashed avocado. Get a container to go (12th and Arch Streets, 625–0321; 4120 Main Street, 930–0272).

HIP FOOD: **Cafe Limbo**, because even those gaunt Generation Xers have to eat sometimes. And surprise—the food's good enough to appeal to baby boomers. Open late; pierced lips optional (2063 South Street, 545–8044).

LIFE-AFFIRMING MEALS: The sleek, calm cafe inside **Essene Natural Foods.** Savory vegetarian fare and a convivial clientele that extends way beyond the Birkenstocked fringe element (719 South 4th Street, 928–3722).

LITERARY DINNERS: The lively French proprietress of **Spring Mill Cafe** hosts regular soirées dedicated to appreciative literary ghosts like Colette and Gertrude Stein (164 Barren Hill Road, Conshohocken, 610–828–2550).

MARTINI: At the elegant **Ritz-Carlton Grill**, there's a whole menu of martini possibilities, stirred or shaken (Liberty Place at 17th and Chestnut Streets, 563–1600).

MEDITERRANEAN UP-AND-COMER: **Dardanelles** is perfect for dining before or after a film at the nearby Ritz theaters. Turkish-born chefs excel at Anatolian salad, the appetizer array called *meze* and grilled fish (213 Chestnut Street, 925–8333).

PLACE TO CELEBRATE YOUR BIRTHDAY: At **Victor Cafe**, the classically trained servers serenade all diners with famous operatic selections. But let them know it's your natal day and they'll harmonize thrillingly on "Happy Birthday." Just don't expect the same virtuosity in the food (1303 Dickinson Street, 468–3040).

RESTAURANT WITH A SOCIAL CONSCIOUSNESS: Splendid breakfasts, big vegetarian platters and free-range chicken are on the menu at the **White Dog Cafe** on the Penn campus, along with a continuing program of speakers on subjects ranging from homelessness to continuing U.S. involvement in Central America. Plus the best block parties in town (3420 Sansom Street, 386–9224).

RESTAURANT FOR GRAZING: Grandiose, marble-pillared **Ciboulette** at the Bellevue, where no dish exceeds $15 and the service and atmosphere are positively blue-chip (200 South Broad Street, 790–1210).

RESTAURANT FOR THE OLD GUARD: Things don't change much at the dignified **Old Guard House Inn**, a Main Line stalwart, and that's just the way conservative patrons like it—prime rib or bust (953 Youngsford Road, Gladwyne, 610–649–9708).

RESTAURANT OVERHAUL: A smart Italian-born chef and a much-needed facelift have breathed new life into Main Line stalwart **Quissett**. And thank God, those spider plants finally died (379 Lancaster Avenue, Haverford, 610–896–0400).

SEVENTIES RESTAURANT: There's a little bit of Haight-Ashbury wiftiness in the air at **Astral Plane**. The kitschy decor, pleasantly throwback grub and mismatched china make you feel like Donovan, Melanie or Tiny Tim might be sitting at the next table (1708 Lombard Street, 546–6230).

SLIM FOOD TO GO: Stop in at **Rittenhouse Grocers** for a tasty 500-calorie dinner-in-a-box that *doesn't* have "deprivation" written all over it. Leftovers, in fact, are a distinct possibility (1934 Rittenhouse Square, 732–6000).

TWIST ON CHEESESTEAK: Cheesesteak soup at the **Pleasant Peasant** is far better than it sounds: a savory take on French *soupe a l'oignon* with melted cheddar and chunks of prime beef (1500 Locust Street, 893–9100).

CHAPTER THREE

Out On the Town and Suburbs:
Philly By Night

O n a good night, Center City hums with action. Smartly dressed throngs milling outside the Academy of Music. The flash of silver cloches whisked off grand dishes at Le Bec-Fin. Poetry readings in dim bars. Carriages drawn through Independence Square by clopping horses. Jazz clubs, neighborhood bars, riverfront mega-nightclubs throbbing with live music and live-wire dancers. In other words, compelling diversions for all tastes in nightlife, especially before the clock strikes midnight.

Bars, Clubs and Dance Floors

A CAPELLA SHOWCASE: Michael's, aswarm with middle-agers reliving their golden years through turgid tunes popularized by the Persuasions and others of their ilk. Actually, once the quintessentially South Philly music starts, the passion for this stuff—both onstage and off—is palpable (239 Chestnut Street, 829–9126).

ACOUSTIC MUSIC: Some good local talent, all quietly unplugged at **Tin Angel**, a mellow, second-story club. Have dinner downstairs at Serrano first (20 South 2nd Street, 928–0978).

BLUES BAR: Shoot some pool, tilt the pinball machine and listen to Elmore James, B.B. King and Billie Holiday on the jukebox at **South Street Blues**, Philly's most traditional blues joint. Live music, too (2100 South Street, 546–9009).

CABARET CLUB: Soul-pop diva and Philly-girl-made-good Patti LaBelle has her own venue, **Chez LaBelle**, with original productions of music, comedy skits and variety acts. Find it in NewMarket, the urban complex off South Street that opened, bombed big-time in the '80s and is supposed to be on its way back (415 South 2nd Street, 1–800–780–6034).

CLUB OF THE MOMENT: Right from the start, **Milkbar Bar & Dancehall** set out to alienate the not-hip-enoughs with a series of provocative ads. As a result, multitudes of the under-30 crowd decided that this former warehouse was *the* cool spot they'd been waiting for, the alternative to Delaware Avenue's raucous, populist clubs (417 North 8th Street, 928–6455).

DANCE BAND: So bursting with brass and soul, you'll find it impossible to keep still once they do your favorite '60s, '70s or '80s tune—that's the thrill of **Johnny O. and the Classic Dogs of Love.** Catch them at bars along the waterfront or in South Philly.

DANCE CLUB: The recently revived **Revival**, which occupies an 1873 former bank-turned-church, is a dramatic venue for cutting-edge dance music. Both DJs and live music—bands from Depeche Mode to Buckwheat Zydeco have performed here—as well as a host of bars, including a '70's retro rec room with an electric flaming fireplace (22 South 3rd Street, 627–4825).

The Library Lounge, where the sophisticated sip.

ENCORE: The return of venerable live-rock venue **Chestnut Cabaret** (3801 Chestnut Street, 386–8555).

FRIDAY HAPPY HOUR: All of those young, upwardly mobile types pour out of the nearby corporate parks to party at **Carolina's Restaurant & Bar** in Radnor. The outdoor seating will help you forget the city's exhaust fumes (333 Belrose Lane, Radnor, 610–293–1000).

GAY BAR, CITY: If you don't have a partner for Two-Step Tuesdays and Super Two-Step Sundays at **Woody's**, well, you'll find one fast (202 South 13th Street, 545–1893).

GAY BAR, COUNTRY: New Hope's famous **Cartwheel**, an old stone mill whose walls now ring with hootin' and hollerin' during drag shows, male stripper performances and dancing to manic DJ music (Route 202, New Hope, 862–0880).

GRUNGE BAR, CITY: Both the old and new meanings of the word "grunge" apply to aptly named **Dirty Frank's**. Don't look for a sign outside—just come on in for a cheap beer and a crush of patrons from all over the city who appreciate the funky vibe of a no-frills bar (13th and Pine Streets, 732–5010).

HAPPY HOUR, CITY: If you just want to have fun, you'll go to Circa. The most *important* bar to hang your elbows on is at the **Palm**—though come to think of it, none of these people look too happy (The Bellevue, Broad and Walnut Streets, 545–7256).

HAPPY HOUR, MAIN LINE: The R5 SEPTA train to Paoli thundering by adds another dimension to the scene at lively Main Line trendcenter **Central Bar & Grille** (39 Morris Avenue, Bryn Mawr, 610–527–1400).

HIGH: The view from the **Eighth Floor** nightclub, a yuppie hotspot with plenty of action (800 North Delaware Avenue, 922–1000).

HORN SECTION: The eight-piece **City Rhythm Orchestra** covers Glenn Miller to Motown with a great, brassy sound. Most recently, they've been Tuesday night regulars at Quincy's in the Adam's Mark Hotel (City Line Avenue at Monument Road, 581–5010).

HOTEL BAR: Like a Main Line mansion, with dark paneling and leather sofas that embrace you as you sink in before a flickering fire on the hearth, the **Library Lounge** inside the Hotel Atop the Bellevue is the coziest, classiest drinking parlor in the city (1415 Chancellor Court at Broad Street, 893–1776).

HOT BLUES CLUB: Check out **Warmdaddy's**, serving up authentic live blues acts and traditional Southern cuisine, from smothered pork chops to chocolate pecan pie (305 South 11th Street, 627–2500).

HOTSPOT: They came, they saw, they conquered. **Circa** is not only the most affordable restaurant that's opened on Walnut Street, but with its elegant atmosphere and "Mike Todd" lounge upstairs, it's the date place Center City has been starving for (1518 Walnut Street, 545–6800).

JAZZ AROUND THE CLOCK: Well, at least once a year, at the **Afro-American Historical and Cultural Museum** for its annual "Jazz 'Til Sunrise" program, featuring Philadelphia's finest internationally acclaimed jazz artists and co-sponsored by PECO (701 Arch Street, 574–3143).

JAZZ BOITE: Slow and easy, when you're in the mood for that, at **Zoot**, a classy newcomer on Headhouse Square (408 South 2nd Street, 925–2590).

JAZZ CLUB, SMOKY: Heavy with atmosphere, **Ortlieb's JazzHaus** is favored by aficionados who believe that the down-and-dirtier the digs, the hotter the music. Excellent Ortlieb's beer on tap, by the way, and an appreciative, involved audience (847 North 3rd Street, 922–1035).

Live jazz at Zanzibar Blue.

JAZZ CLUB, UPSCALE: Philly nightlife gets a brassy boost from **Zanzibar Blue**, featuring live jazz by the city's finest seven nights a week in a classy restaurant-*cum*-bar (301 South 11th Street, 829–0300).

For the latest on live tunes in Philadelphia, check the listings in the weekend section of the daily newspaper, or in the weekly *City Paper* and *Philadelphia Weekly*.

JAZZ JAM SESSION: Young men tooting their own horns and other amateur performers join the action onstage every Tuesday night at the **23rd Street Cafe** (23 North 23rd Street, 561–2488).

JAZZ WORKSHOPS: Affiliated with a community center established in the late '60s to help heal the ravages of gang warfare and bring people together through jazz, the **Mill Creek Jazz and Cultural Society** is a gem for buffs (Jazz Loft at Mill Creek, 4624 Lancaster Avenue, 473–4273).

JITTERBUGGING: With a no-alcohol, no-smoking, no-high-heels policy and cookies baked by its members for refreshments, the **Philadelphia Swing Dance Society** redefines the meaning of good clean fun. Call to find out where they're currently getting together (6815 Emlen Street, 576–0345).

JUKEBOX, CITY: The one at **Tavern on Green**, programmed by long-time barkeep Jim Anderson, is refreshingly schizophrenic, crammed with tunes by Peggy Lee, the Bay City Rollers, Donny Osmond, Eydie Gorme, the Meat Puppets, Frank Sinatra and a few of our favorite selections from *The Sound of Music* (21st and Green Streets, 235–6767).

JUKEBOX, SOUTH JERSEY: There's barbecue good enough to satisfy a born-and-bred Southerner, and all manner of vintage blues ballads on the jukebox at **Red, Hot and Blue**, right across the street from the Garden State Racetrack (Route 70 and Sayre Road, Cherry Hill, 609–665–7427).

LINE DANCING: Been sleeping single in a double bed? Or secretly watching TNN music videos? Mosey over and join in the line dances at **Bronko Bill's** in the Great Northeast, a country-music entertainment complex so vast it approaches Dollywood proportions (Grant Avenue and Bluegrass Road, 677–8700).

MARTINIS: **Morton's of Chicago.** With a special menu listing 40 variations on the theme, they've forged the commitment to serve a perfect one. On second thought, make that a Bombay Sapphire (1 Logan Square, 557–0724).

NEIGHBORHOOD BAR: **Chris'** cafe, where owner Chris Dhmitri only needs to meet you once to greet you by name forever after. Live jazz, every night, with no cover charge (1421 Sansom Street, 568–3131).

Cowboy boots were made for two-steppin' at Bronko Bill's.

Verse Chic:
The Best Places to Hear, See and Do Poetry

In the '70s, sensitive troubadors monopolized open-mike night at the local bar. In the '80s, stand-up comics took over. Now, poetic justice beckons versiphiles of all ages, either to read or listen as others spill their literary guts.

POETRY ACTIVISTS: Ever since the film *Dead Poets Society* made verse readings trendy again, the **Philomathean Society** at the University of Pennsylvania has sponsored "Keats and Beats" meetings. Members have also held "drive-by" readings, shouting poetry while riding their bikes through the city (College Hall, 34th and Locust Streets, 898–8907).

VISIONARY POETRY READING SPOT: North Star Bar, a favored music venue, has been holding poetry readings for the past ten years, long before it became a mainstream hip thing to do (27th and Poplar Streets, 235–7827).

POETRY VENUE FOR SCAREDY CATS: Bring your tortured thoughts to cozy **Doc Watson's Pub** on Monday nights. The crowd's exceptionally polite and respectful (216 South 11th Street, 922–3427).

FRIDAY NIGHT READINGS: A comfy-as-an-old-shoe place like the **City Book Shop** could become one's whole social life, what with featured poets reading every Friday night throughout the year (1129 Pine Street, 592–1992).

GROUP FOR ASPIRING POETS: Poets and Prophets, a "freelance" poetry group, arranges a monthly menu of readings at

Borders Book Shop. Check the shop's monthly newsletter for appearances by poets of national renown (1727 Walnut Street, 568–7400).

GRUNGE POETRY READINGS: In collaboration with the *Painted Bride Quarterly*, issued by the famed Philly performance space of the same name, the **Last Drop Coffeehouse** holds poetry readings with writers who are quite full of themselves (13th and Pine Streets, 893–0434).

PLACE TO POSE, ARTSY: The Arts Bank's **Cafe des Artistes** is a nightly parade of, well, *unusual* types from University of the Arts and beyond. Naturally, everyone smokes, but there is a lovely variety of teas and pleasant staff—plus monthly poetry recitals (601 South Broad Street, 545–4580).

RETRO LOUNGE: Would-be Warhols can wear their black turtle-necks and wax cynical amid the fabulous '50's furniture and kick-ass rock music at the **Silk City Lounge**, next door to the funky American Diner (5th and Spring Garden Streets, 592–8838).

REVIVAL: Revival. One of the city's most durable dance clubs has come back into fashion after a recent facelift (22 South 3rd Street, 627–4825).

SATURDAY NIGHT DATE SPOT: At the aptly named **Love Lounge**, above the Knave of Hearts restaurant, you'll find campy decor, puffy sofas for smooching and libations ranging from coffee to a passion-fruit "Love Potion #9" (232 South Street, 922–3956).

SHOT AND A BEER: At the polished bar inside **Jack's Firehouse**, the upscale restaurant across from historic Eastern State Penitentiary. Plenty of joints serve boutique beers, but chef Jack McDavid brews his own lightning-hot moonshine whiskey (shh . . . it's a secret!) and stocks a connoisseur's choice of bitchin' sour-mash bourbon (2130 Fairmount Avenue, 232–9000).

SHOT, IF YOU DARE: **Mako's Retired Surfers' Bar & Grill**, a surfer-themed foodrinkery, proffers a full spectrum of jello shots in lurid blues and greens. These jiggly confections had their hey-day a couple of years ago, but here they wiggle on. Since South Street is the Boardwalk of Philly, there's no more appropriate place in town to suck one down (48–50 South Street, 625–3820).

SOCIAL CLIMBERS' BAR: One flight of floridly carpeted stairs down from vaunted haute cuisine parlor Le Bec-Fin is chef Georges Perrier's vision of the perfect bar: **Le Bar Lyonnais**.

Tenebrous and intimate, serving chic little plates of oysters, it's the best spot in town to sip a flute of champagne with someone you want to impress (1523 Walnut Street, 567–1000).

SPORTS BAR: **Legends at the Holiday Inn at the Stadium,** a pop fly from the Vet and the Spectrum. Not only does it have the requisite multiple television monitors (41 of them), it's also the best place to see professional athletes unwinding after a game. But if Jim Fregosi is there hunched over a newspaper and the Phillies just lost, do the poor guy a favor and leave him alone (10th Street and Packer Avenue, 755–9500).

SQUARE DANCING: For dyed-in-the-wool do-si-doers or the merely curious, hoedowns at **Club Sashay** prove square dancing isn't just for squares. They usually meet at the Hancock Methodist Church in Springfield (610–566–6552).

TOUCH DANCING, CITY: The **Barrymore Room** inside Philly's venerable Hotel Atop the Bellevue is a dreamy venue for dancing in the dark on Friday and Saturday evenings (1415 Chancellor Court at Broad Street, 790–2814).

TOUCH DANCING, SUBURBS: The **Washington Crossing Inn** in Bucks County has cha-cha and fox-trotting to a big band on Friday and Saturday nights. Congenial older crowd, as might be expected (Routes 532 and 32, Washington Crossing, 493–3634).

Delaware Avenue:
Philly's Nightclub Strip

Funseekers lurching from dance club to burger joint to parking lot, cars whizzing over potholes as music churns in the not-too-distant background. Though they are a mecca for the young and restless, the clubs of Delaware Avenue—renamed Columbus Boulevard in honor of the Italian explorer, but popularly known by its old name—are for anyone who wants to dance, hear live music and flirt like crazy.

FIRST REASON TO VISIT THE AVENUE: For the mild but legitimate thrill of being right alongside the mighty **Delaware River,** the third longest river in the East, with all the vague romanticism implied. But please, watch out for the traffic.

SECOND REASON TO VISIT THE AVENUE: There's fierce competition among waterfront clubs to book the most popular groups, but **Katmandu Village** alternates reggae acts with bands that could just as easily take the stage at "real" music venues. The tropical, Club Med-esque joint also seems to attract a more diverse clientele than its neighbors. Two restaurants, six bars and a piano lounge (Pier 25, 417 North Delaware Avenue, 629–7400).

MEAL ON THE AVENUE: **La Veranda** has absolutely nothing to do with the nightclub scene. It's an old-time Italian restaurant with deferential waiters, very good pasta, a nice antipasto selection and, depending on where you sit, a tranquil view of the marina (Pier 3, Penn's Landing at Arch Street, 351–1898).

Look both ways when crossing Delaware Avenue on foot, especially on busy weekend nights. The traffic can be just as wild as the clubs!

SHOWERS: Two blocks north of Spring Garden Street, the Beach Club, now operating as **Bahama Bay,** is Philly's only true alfresco club, with tons of sand imported to create a beach on the fragrant Delaware banks. After lounging in the sun or smacking a volleyball, those outdoor showers come in pretty handy (Pier 42, 945 North Delaware Avenue, 829–9799).

MARTINI: Grown-up drinks are rare hereabouts, where the beer flows like—well, beer—but they'll mix yours stirred, not shaken, at the **Eighth Floor.** What this relatively civilized club lacks in decorative panache, it makes up for with a stunning view of the Benjamin Franklin Bridge by night—and an improbably thrilling ride up to the bar in an old freight elevator (800 North Delaware Avenue, 922–1000).

IMITATION OF A NEW YORK CLUB: Definitely not for inhibited types, **Planet Rock** features house, club and techno music—the meaning of which is difficult to pin down, but which implies mosh pits, flashing and other transcendent group experiences. It's one of three clubs in this com-

Dave & Buster's is an arcade for kids of all ages.

plex—the others are **Voodoo** and the **Cave** (700 North Delaware Avenue, 923–0504).

VIRTUAL REALITY: Don that helmet and you're on the superhighway to other worlds at mega-club **Dave & Buster's**. A phalanx of pool tables, games, arcade extraordinaire, high-decibel bar, decent burgers at the Bridgeside Grill—all this, and escapism, too (Pier 19 North, 325 North Delaware Avenue, 413–1951).

ALTERNATIVE TO DAVE & BUSTER'S FOR POOL TABLES: Tired of waiting for your turn to break? Take your cue and head over to the **Riverbank Entertainment Center**, where 34 tables await. The owners plan to expand with a game center, espresso bar and just what the area needs—another club (800 North Delaware Avenue, 925–1820).

MAINSTREAM ALTERNATIVE: The people who hang out at **Egypt** take pains to differentiate themselves from the cheesier element that frequents the other clubs. With features like a Tuesday "Asian night," it also makes an effort to attract clubgoers from China-town and other parts of the city, instead of just

Take your mummy to Egypt on Delaware Avenue.

the "bridge and tunnel crowd" (Delaware Avenue and Spring Garden Street, 922–6500).

OLDIES: You may not know Nirvana from Nine-Inch Nails, but you're never too old to shake, rattle and do

the mashed potato at **Rock Lobster**. Pleasant, seashorey decor under a pair of giant circus tents and, depending on the night, decent grilled lobster (Delaware Avenue at Vine Street, 627–ROCK).

WATERFRONT VIEW:

Crustaceans welcome you to Rock Lobster on the Delaware River.

What a way to get away—you really feel *on* the river at the former **Eli's Pier 34**, now known as the **Blu Water Cafe**, just south of Penn's Landing. More of a restaurant than a mere meat market, it lures a democratic mix of ages and appetites (Fitzwater Street at Delaware Avenue, 923–2500).

WAY TO GET AROUND: When crossing Delaware Avenue, pedestrians take their lives in their own hands. That's what makes the **Water Taxi** so appealing—go club-hopping via the Delaware River, not Avenue. These 26-foot crafts will take you one way for $3, and offer a $5 all-day, all-night open ticket (Call 800–255–0256, ext. 44221 to page the Water Taxi, or pick it up at Penn's Landing or at any of the clubs).

The Performing Arts

ALTERNATIVE THEATER: The **Freedom Repertory Theatre** presents powerful dramas and readings based on the black experience, as well as speakers featuring African-American playwrights from Langston Hughes to Ntozake Shange (1346 North Broad Street, 765–2793).

ANACHRONISTIC PERFORMANCE SPACE: Built in 1911, **Plays and Players Theatre** is a creaky old space that reeks with old-money character. Established for society's hoi polloi, it now sees several plays a year, and is frequently the scene of benefit parties and other Rittenhouse Square social events (1714 Delancey Street, 735–0630).

AUDIENCE PARTICIPATION: The annual "all people's hanging out together, singing, eating, music, dancing and theater free fest" at the **People's Light & Theater Company**, located inside an old stone barn (39 Conestoga Road, Malvern, 451–7777).

CHORAL GROUP: For more than 20 years, the **Philadelphia Singers** have been performing the music of J.S. Bach in a rousing, joyous style that's been called "Dixieland Bach." They often appear at Rittenhouse Square's Church of the Holy Trinity (751–9494).

COMMUNITY THEATER IN THE CITY: Giving the Painted Bride a run for its money in the eclectic department, the **Actors' Center Theater** at the Bourse offers a full schedule including New York City cabaret performers, children's theater, art exhibits, play readings and premieres of local films—*plus* dessert and cappuccino (21 South 5th Street, 928–0404).

DANCE PERFORMANCE: **Philadelphia Dance Company**, better known as **Philadanco**, celebrates the black experience—via music from Otis Redding to Bach—through ballet and contemporary movement. Actually, the troupe is onstage in Philly less and less frequently, spending most of its time teaching and touring. Catch them in town at the Zellerbach Theater at the Annenberg Center (3680 Walnut Street, 387–8200).

The Freedom Repertory Theatre's Barrymore Award nominated, annual holiday production, *Black Nativity*.

FREE CLASSICAL CONCERTS: The **Curtis Institute of Music** presents excellent free student recitals two or three times a week during the academic year. But go ahead and splurge on tickets to its Symphony Orchestra performances, too (1726 Locust Street, 893–5261).

HALF-PRICE TICKETS: The day of performance *only*, and no mail orders. You can call **Upstages** to check on availability, but must pick up the tickets in person, either at the Upstages booth on the second floor of Liberty Place, 17th and Chestnut Streets, adjacent to the food court, or inside the Philadelphia Arts Bank, 601 South Broad Street (893–1145).

INTELLECTUAL THEATER: No sugar-coated musicals or feel-good plays at the **Wilma Theater**, founded by Czech emigres Jiri and Blanka Zizka. This challenging company favors edgy Euro-works by the likes of Vaclav Havel and Athol Fugard (2030 Sansom Street, 963–0345).

LAWRENCE WELK REVIVALS: Now, that's not really fair, because Johnny Cash or jazz-hot Spiro Gyra are just as likely to be on the bill at the **Keswick Theatre**. But during the holiday season, those who miss the Lennon sisters can swing to that polka beat again (Easton Road and Keswick Avenue, Glenside, 572–7650).

NEW THEATER EXPERIENCE: PAPA (Philadelphia Alliance for Performance Alternatives) brings cutting edge *artistes* to Philly—slash artist Ron Athey, vulgarian Annie Sprinkle—and produces local artists like Elizabeth Smullens, who charmed, startled and shook us up in May with her "Wizard of Oz"-themed act. Look for PAPA starting again in September (925–PAPA).

OPERA: The **Academy of Vocal Arts Opera Theatre** performs classics round the city and into Bucks County: Verdi, Mozart, Humperdinck (Humperdinck?). Its regular concert extravaganzas feature a glowing coterie of opera stars, many of them AVA alumni (735–1685).

SEAL OF APPROVAL FOR THEATERGOERS: The **Barrymore Awards**, a program of the Performing Arts League of Philadelphia (PALP) that recognizes excellence in theater. Before you call for tickets, dial the PALP hotline at 573–ARTS.

SEAT AT THE ACADEMY OF MUSIC: The best sound is beneath

the stage, where melodies swell to maximum glory. But for an excellent ground-floor vantage point, try to get seats just behind the orchestra, in front of the last row of box seats (Broad and Locust Streets, 893–1999).

SHAKESPEARE INTERPRETATIONS: By turns tender, humorous, slightly shocking and just original enough, at the earnest young **Arden Theatre Company**. Most performances are at the intimate St. Stephen's Alley Performing Arts Centre (10th and Ludlow Streets, 829–8900).

The curtain isn't the only thing going up at the Koresh Dance Center.

URBAN DANCE PERFORMANCE: Everything from hip-hop and jazz to modern and balletic moves at the modest **Koresh Dance Center**, home of the troupe by the same name (104 South 20th Street, 751–0959).

Film

ART FILMS, CITY: Our two beloved Ritz theaters—the **Ritz at the Bourse**, and the **Ritz Five**—are well-oiled film machines. If only more theaters sold biscotti, fresh coffee and herbal tea to help you stay awake during those Chinese subtitles (Look for a new Ritz at the Main Street complex in Voorhees, New Jersey.) (4th and Ranstead Streets, 925–7900; 214 Walnut Street, 925–7900).

ART FILMS, SUBURBS: Anticipation builds as you approach the handsome, yellow-and-blue **County Theater** in Doylestown. Inside, it's a pristinely preserved vintage space from the grand days of cinema, offering all the niceties of the Ritzes, plus an engaging newsletter (20 East State Street, Doylestown, 348–3456).

DRIVE-IN THEATER: And you thought they'd all gone the way of Sal Mineo. For nostalgic viewing, or to show the kids what it was all about, drive up to Bucks County for double features at the **Bucks County Drive-In** (Route 611 near Willow Grove, 343–8641).

GENERAL-RELEASE MOVIE THEATER: The lobby's so luxuriantly huge you'll wonder why they didn't allot a little more space for actual viewing. Still, the United Artists **Riverview Plaza Theatre** is a treat for residents who want to see the newest Schwarzenegger release and would rather avoid Center City (1400 South Delaware Avenue, 755–2219).

MOVIE THEATER FOR ALIENATED 15-YEAR-OLDS ON THEIR FIRST DATE: Of all places, the Franklin Institute, whose **Tuttleman Omniverse Theater** shows in-your-face laser movies of rock groups —far more sophisticated than mere MTV videos—on its enormous screen. Led Zeppelin's *Lased and Confused* is a fave (Benjamin Franklin Parkway at 20th Street, 448–1388).

POST-MOVIE SNACKING, CENTER CITY: It's *amore* pie at **Cafe Casa Nova**, in the same strip mall as Riverview Plaza—noisy, but pleasant, dependable and kid-friendly (1400 South Delaware Avenue, 463–7707).

POST-MOVIE SNACKING, 'BURBS: It's worth taking in a movie at the nice, clean, suburban Narberth theater so you can visit the cozy **Balcony Cafe** right next door (125 North Narberth Avenue, Narberth, 610–664–8211).

SEASONAL TREAT FOR FILM BUFFS: It's not yet ranked with Cannes or Sundance, but the **Philadelphia Festival of World Cinema** in the spring has grown steadily over the last few years, attracting films from Europe and the Far East. Showings are at area theaters (895–6593).

VINTAGE MOVIE THEATER: Few cinemas hold such promise as the gorgeous, overtly ornate **Anthony Wayne**, with its facade of brilliantly tiled foofaraw (109 West Lancaster Avenue, Wayne, 610–688–0800).

....

Information, Please:
Museums and Institutions

AIDS RESOURCE: Our **AIDS Information Network** was the country's first lending library dedicated to information on AIDS and the HIV virus from sources around the world, and remains one of the most comprehensive (1211 Chestnut Street, 922–5120).

ART EXPERIENCE: The **Institute of Contemporary Art**, administered by the University of Pennsylvania, is a nonprofit, noncollecting exhibition space dedicated to presenting "the art of our time." With more than 10,000 square feet of gallery space for lectures, performances, symposia and films, it's the best venue in town for exploring today's multi-faceted contemporary art scene (118 South 18th Street, 898–7108).

Ken Moody and Robert Sherman, 1984 was highlighted at Robert Mapplethorpe's groundbreaking 1988–1989 exhibit at the Institute of Contemporary Art.

BOOKLOVERS' LIBRARY: Seek inspiration in an original manuscript of **Ulysses** (if you can decipher James Joyce's minuscule, cramped handwriting) and pore over moving missals penned by some of Philadelphia's founding mothers at the **Rosenbach Museum and Library** (2010 Delancey Street, 732–1600).

ETHNIC MUSEUM: A great place for kids, full of folkloric designs and appealing exhibits on Russian culture and fairy tales, the **Polish American Cultural Center Museum** may be close to Independence Square, but it transports a visitor worlds away (308 Walnut Street, 922–1700).

GIFT SHOP IN A MUSEUM: Not to say that the 30 galleries of materials from ancient Egypt, Mesopotamia, Mesoamerica, Asia and the Greco-Roman world aren't terribly impressive, it's just that the selection of jewelry and gifts at the Museum Shop at the **University of Pennsylvania Museum of Archaeology and Anthropology** is compelling enough to attract visitors in its *own* right (33rd and Spruce Streets, 898–4000).

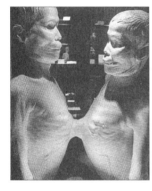

HUMAN ORGAN, REAL: Talk about gross anatomy! The **Mütter Museum** is a showplace of flesh-and-blood specimens removed from patients during the 19th century, when physicians were learning new techniques for treating illness. It's all pretty graphic, but squeamish types seem to cringe the most at the sight of that double liver removed from the famous Siamese twins, Chang and Eng (College of Physicians and Surgeons, 19 South 22nd Street, 563–3737).

Siamese twins Chang and Eng at the Mutter Museum, which documents three centuries of medicine in Philadelphia.

HUMAN ORGAN, REPLICA: The heart at the **Franklin Institute**, a low-tech thrill for both kids and adults who recall it from their own childhood. This four-ton papier-mâché replica was meant to be a temporary exhibit, but once Philadelphians got inside, there was no tearing it down. Today, closed-circuit TVs deter potential vein vandals with arterial motives (20th Street and the Benjamin Franklin Parkway, 448–1200).

LIBRARY BRANCH: There's no browsing in the stacks, but the efficient computer service at the original **Free Library of Philadelphia** almost atones for the fact that you can't really lose yourself in this elephantine edifice, designed by the estimable Horace Trumbauer and built in 1917 (19th and Vine Streets, 686–5407).

MUSEUM DATE: The **Rodin Museum** is small and intimate, as romantic as the Art Museum on a Wednesday night, but far less crowded. Contemplate *The Thinker* and the *Gates of Hell* (26th Street and the Benjamin Franklin Parkway, 763–8100).

The Franklin Institute has four floors of exhibits, plus the Mandell Future Center and the Tuttleman Omniverse Theater.

MUSEUM FOR VIKING FANS: Located incongruously in the heart of Italian South Philadelphia, the **American Swedish Historical Museum** is a giddy 1930's recreation of Sweden's Eriksberg Castle. Check out the rooms full of Viking memorabilia, and the gallery modeled after an Art Deco smoking lounge from a Swedish ocean liner (1900 Pattison Avenue, 389–1776).

MUSEUM IN A SYNAGOGUE: The permanent collection of the **National Museum of American Jewish History** contains more than 7,500 objects documenting three centuries of Jewish culture in America. It shares space with Congregation Mikveh Israel, the country's second oldest continuing congregation,

A samovar on exhibit at the National Museum of American Jewish History, the only museum of its kind in the country.

which presents a Sephardic service virtually unchanged since the 18th century (55 North 5th Street, 923–3812).

MUSEUM WHERE YOU CAN LEARN A NEW DANCE STEP: At the impossibly showy **New Year's Shooters and Mummers Museum**, you'll read all sorts of high-minded explanations for the phenomenon of grown men who spend their free time wearing feathers and sequins, playing funny music, and parading through Center City on New Year's Day. It all dates back to the 1700s, when the bands' "instruments" were loaded pistols, today, it's just good-natured New Year's revelry. Consult the exhibit in the lobby to learn the famed Mummers "strut" and the Cakewalk (1100 South 2nd Street, 336–3050).

NUMISMATICIANS' THRILL: The **United States Mint**, the largest mint in the world, boasts a well-stocked gift shop and two fabulous glass mosaics by Louis Comfort Tiffany. Perhaps its most stunning feature is the 150-year-old stuffed eagle, purportedly the model for the American eagle that appeared on our old silver coins (5th and Arch Streets, 597–7350).

PRISON TOURS: The Louvre, Versailles, the Vatican . . . you've seen it all. But have you ever been to prison? Tour the **Eastern State Penitentiary** National Historic Monument, which Al Capone and Willie Sutton called home. Guided hardhat tours include visits to the cell blocks, prison greenhouse and death row (22nd Street and Fairmount Avenue, 236–7326).

The Civil War Library and Museum, founded in 1888, was first presided over by Rutherford B. Hayes.

VICTORIANA: Whether you own a house as fabulous and floral as this 1814 Italian Renaissance Revival brownstone, or just daydream about redecorating in grand old style, it's worth a visit to the **Athenaeum of Philadelphia**. Interior designers often stop by the Victorian Society of America headquarters inside to check out the latest exhibit (219 South 6th Street, 925–2688).

PLACE TO SEE A DEAD HORSE: His head is all that remains of Old Baldy, beloved steed that Union officer George Gordon

Meade rode into battle. See it, and much more, at our own **Civil War Library and Museum** (1805 Pine Street, 735–8196).

PLACE TO TAKE A EUROPEAN GUEST: The **Philadelphia Museum of Art**! One of the world's great art institutions, it's a repository of innumerable treasures, including Cezanne's *Grandes Baigneuses* ("Big Bathers"), van Goghs and Renoirs (26th Street and Benjamin Franklin Parkway, 763–8100).

MUSEUM IN A FURNESS BUILDING: The quietly alluring **Samuel S. Fleisher Art Memorial** in a church designed by famed Philadelphia architect Frank Furness and completed in 1886. Highlights include a

> **The Philadelphia Museum of Art, housed here since 1928, has more than 300,000 works of art.**

magnificent altarpiece by Brandywine School artist Violet Oakley, and some breathtaking stained glass (709–721 Catharine Street, 922–3456).

MUSEUM DEDICATED TO A MOVIE STAR: South of South Street, at the Settlement Music School in residential Queen Village, the **Mario Lanza Museum** is dedicated to the second-rate opera singer and bona fide film legend—most notably, star of the 1951 classic *The Great Caruso* (416 Queen Street, 468–3623).

TEXTILE ARTISTRY: Always captivating and sometimes shocking, the pieces displayed at the **Fabric Workshop** stand boldly on the cutting edge of fabric design. Resident artists accomplished in other media work along with students, and the results—take one home from the small museum shop—are highly distinctive (1315 Cherry Street, 922–7303).

The Red Madrass Headdress is one of 60 Matisse works at the Barnes Foundation.

STAMP-COLLECTOR'S THRILL: The United States Postal Service Museum also displays Pony Express pouches and original copies of the *Pennsylvania Gazette* published by Benjamin Franklin, who—among myriad other pursuits—happens to have been the country's first Postmaster General (Franklin Court, Market Street between South 3rd and 4th Streets, 597–8974).

TV WEATHERCAST: While Channel 10 tries to dazzle us with Earthwatch (not to mention John Bolaris), and Channel 3 touts "Doppler Radar," Action News uses a weather chart that looks like it belongs in a preschool—big yellow smiley-face suns, mean frowning clouds—and still kicks ass in ratings.

WORLD-CLASS ART COLLECTION: Pharmaceutical magnate Dr. Albert C. Barnes, who died in 1951, amassed one of the most distinguished collections of 19th and 20th century art—including works by Cezanne, Renoir, Matisse and their distinguished peers—which he had mounted in an extremely eccentric manner in his personal gallery. Now open to the public, the Barnes Foundation finds an aesthetic setting in its 12-acre arboretum, designed in 1933, which is a treat for horticulture buffs as well (300 North Latch's Lane, Merion, 610–667–0290).

Fun and Games

BASKETBALL COURT: Suburban schoolyards are great, and the Sporting Club at the Bellevue does nicely for upscale bouts of pickup, but all savvy city shooters know Palumbo Playground has a well-maintained wooden floor in the sunken court, as gratifying for the spectators as it is for the slam-dunkers themselves. Also a nice neighborhood scene, come summer (9th and Bainbridge Streets).

BATTING CAGES: Swing for all you're worth at Grand Slam U.S.A. Don't worry—you won't be the only adult waiting his turn for one of this fun center's six cages (Lancaster Pike and Route 29, Malvern, 610–647–6622).

BILLIARDS PARLOR, PHILLY: A neighborhood hangout during the week, **River City Billiards** turns into a cool date destination on weekends in chicer-by-the-moment Manayunk (4258 Main Street, 482–7410).

BILLIARDS PARLOR, SOUTH JERSEY: Clean, upscale, Art Deco-and-neon **Breakers**, conveniently connected to the Playdrome bowling alley (King's Highway and Ellisburg Circle, Cherry Hill, NJ, 609–795–5458).

Take your cue and head over to Breakers.

BOWLING: Even proper Main Line types feel the need to hurl those heavy balls down the alley sometimes. And they have the most civilized place to do it in: **Devon Lanes** (300 Lancaster Avenue, Devon, 610–688–1920).

BOWLING, SOUTH JERSEY: Clean, upscale, Art Deco-and-neon **Playdrome Cherry Hill** is spiffy, yes, but a bowling alley nonetheless (King's Highway and Ellisburg Circle, Cherry Hill, NJ, 609–429–0672).

DARTS, CITY: Have a superb, crafted-on-premises beer in this upmarket microbrewery, and challenge one of those callow young lawyers to hit the bullseye, at **Dock Street Brewery and Restaurant** (2 Logan Square, 496–0413).

DARTS, 'BURBS: Its ads promise "No bozos," but of course, that's all in the eye of the beholder. Meanwhile, **Butler's Pub** boasts its own parking lot *and* a serious darts scene—both de rigueur for the civilized life in Chestnut Hill (21 West Highland Avenue, 247–3249).

GAMBLING: The **Turf Club**, a bona fide, brass-rail betting parlor, features live broadcasts for those who can't make it out to the horsetrack. A lively scene that can be fun as long as you don't enjoy it *too* much (Penn Center, 17th and Market Streets, 246–1556, 2200 Packer Avenue, 246–1556).

SPORTS TALK SHOW: Okay, so nobody's listening, but you won't hear **Neil Hartman** of fledgling sports yakker WGMP 1210 AM dressing down callers and labeling players "stinkin' losers." You will, however, hear insightful questions put to sports news-makers. And though Howard Eskin promotes himself as Charles Barkley's confidant, Hartman really is Sir Charles's best friend.

The Active Life:
Out and About

BIKE RENTAL, CITY: Whether you're planning to tool around Penn's Landing or pedal ambitiously through Fairmount Park, **Bike Line** rents mountain bikes for $15 a day (13th and Locust Streets, 735–1503).

BIKE RENTAL, SUBURBS: Helmet up and take to those suburban slopes—**Erdenheim Bicycle Center** rents mountain bikes for $30 a day (821 Bethlehem Pike, Erdenheim, 233–3883).

BIKERS' TRIUMPH: Thanks to the efforts of the feisty **Bicycle Coalition of the Delaware Valley**, you can take your bicycle on SEPTA and PATCO trains, and therefore ride anywhere from the green suburbs of the Main Line to the streets of Atlantic City (829–4188).

GOLF COURSE, PUBLIC: There's no membership necessary to hit the links at the **Waynesborough Country Club**, but don't kid yourself— if you're not from the Main Line, they'll know (610–296–2131).

GOLF COURSE, MINIATURE: The best ones are at the shore, of course, but those with the urge for a round of pitch-n-putt would do well to check out **Woody's**, with a bargain price of $3.25 for nine holes of play (559 Germantown Avenue, Norristown, 610–279–0678).

HAYRIDES: Head out to the great pumpkin patch to pluck your own jack-o-lantern, pick some apples off a tree or just snuggle in the hay with your companions at **Conte's Orchards** (Flyatt Road, Tabernacle, NJ, 609–268–1010).

HEALTH CLUB RIVALRY: Brand new **Bally's Holiday Fitness Center** vs. the Sporting Club. That rug is getting pretty ragged at the Sporting Club, guys (1500 Market Street, 665–9777).

JOGGING PATHS: It's hard to believe that the bucolic splendor of **Forbidden Drive**, which winds alongside the charming Valley Green Inn in Chestnut Hill, is actually within city limits.

MOUNTAIN-CLIMBING INSTRUCTION: Harness up, and then—to the sound of blaring rock-and-roll—dauntingly muscled teachers at the **Philadelphia Rock Gym**, near Valley Forge Park, will help you learn to scale the indoor, *American Gladiators*-style wall. Outdoor instruction is provided, as well. Prepare to ache tomorrow (Route 422, Oaks, 610–666–ROPE).

PLACE TO GO ON A BEAUTIFUL DAY: **Bartram's Garden**, the 18th-century horticultural proving ground complete with wildflower meadow and coach house complex (54th Street and Lindbergh Boulevard, 729–5281).

Check out Philadelphia from a whole new angle, whether catching a breeze aboard a sailboat or lounging on a cruise ship. The Delaware River takes on a majesty all its own as you drift away from the city.

RIDING STABLES: Lessons with patient instructors and even more patient beasts of burden are available at **Gateway Stables**. If you already know how to ride, harness up and go for miles on the quiet trails (Marybell Lane, Kennett Square, 610–444–9928).

POLO, MAIN LINE: Refreshments are served during games at the **Brandywine Polo Club**, whose season runs from Memorial Day weekend through late September. Bouts take place on Sundays in season at 3 p.m., at various fields throughout the verdant Main Line. Spectators are welcome (610–444–1582 or 610–268–8692).

Horse play at the Brandywine Polo Club.

POLO, BUCKS COUNTY: There's down-to-earth tailgate picnicking and plenty of action at **Bucks County Polo Club.** Matches are open to the public on Sundays at 1 p.m. from spring through fall (Bucks County Horse Park, Route 611 between Revere and Ferndale, 610–847–8228).

SAILING: Although its name suggests a place for the rich and famous, the **Liberty Yacht Club and Sailing School** offers classes of various levels, and permits members with significant sailing experience to take a sailboat out on the river unsupervised. Even if you're not into learning, it's a great place to hop a short river cruise on a hot night (Pier 12, 235 North Columbus Boulevard, 922–4005).

SPORTING GOODS FIND: Play it Again, Sports: Retread golf clubs, soccer shoes, baseball gloves and hockey skates, since you and your kids are just going to outgrow them or slice into the woods with them anyway (500 Baltimore Pike, Springfield, 610–543–2008; 1149 Lancaster Avenue, Rosemont Square, Rosemont, 610–519–9530).

TESTOSTERONE SPECIAL: Friday night at Philly's premier pugilistic parlor, the **Blue Horizon.** The sweat, the steam, the danger . . . a great aphrodisiac, for those outside the ring, anyway (1314 North Broad Street, 763–0500).

UNDERATTENDED SPORT: The Spectrum crowds may be smaller for the **Bulldogs,** Philly's roller hockey team, than they are for the Flyers, but the screaming's just as loud (389–9595).

WAY TO MEET FELLOW HIKERS: Hiking may strike some as a solitary sport, but members of the **Wanderlust Clubhikes** enjoy each other's company while roaming Forbidden Drive, down along the Wissahickon Creek to Valley Green (580–4847).

After Midnight:
Late-Night Philly

At the murky edge of the evening, when you're desperate for a magazine, sustenance, company or even a Xerox machine, there are places in the city and surroundings where a night-owl can roost.

BOOKSTORE: Check out **Afterwords** for a browsable, thoughtful selection of contemporary fiction, foreign periodicals, gifts and gay lit. And it's open until 11 p.m. on weekdays, 3 a.m. on weekends (218 South 12th Street, 735–2393).

BOWLING: Go for strikes and spares until the pre-wee hours at **Boulevard Lanes**—a real old-fashioned "neighborhood" bowling alley in the heart of the Great Northeast with recently refurbished lanes and a friendly atmosphere. The fun ends at 2 a.m. weekends, 11 p.m. weekdays (8011 Roosevelt Blvd., 332–9200).

BREAKFAST: Oatmeal is your safest bet at the diner-like dive **Little Pete's**, a little slice of *Midnight Cowboy* right in Center City (219 South 17th Street, 545–5508).

BREAKFAST AFTER THE GAY BARS CLOSE: The cruising slows down, but never really stops at the genially hip, low-key eatery **Duck Soup**. Do yourself a favor, though, and resist the oleaginous French fries (267 South 12th Street, 735–6650).

BURGER: It's business as usual 24 hours on weekends, until midnight the rest of the time at Philly's two **American Diners**. They attract students and artist-types, all crowding into the scarlet booths for a better hamburger and fries than you have a right to expect at this hour—whatever this hour may be (6th and Spring Garden Streets, 592–8838; 4201 Chestnut Street, 387–1451).

CHEESESTEAK, SOUTH PHILLY: Pat's King of Steaks, the beloved cheesesteakerie. "Extraordinary," say some aficionados, kissing their greasy fingertips. Others favor the similarly non-nutritive belly bombs at Geno's, just across 9th Street (1237 East Passyunk Avenue, 468–1546).

CHEESESTEAK, UNIVERSITY CITY: Students at Penn and Drexel eat enough cheesesteaks to know what's good. Their local best: **Billybob's**, where the atmo's properly seedy and the televisions are always blaring. Try the cheese fries (4000 Spruce Street, 222–4340).

COCKTAILS AT 4 A.M.: When you can't afford to be fussy, stop at one of Center City's **Midtown** restaurants, owned and operated by the Hionas family. Each is complete with cocktail lounge, bakery and plenty of cigarette smoke (**Midtown II**, 122 South 11th Street, 627–6452; **Midtown IV**, 2013 Chestnut Street, 567–3142).

COPIES: *Must* have that resume for tomorrow? *Forgot* all about your wedding invitations? **Kinko's** makes color copies, prints resumes and rents IBM and Mac computers—around the clock (3923 Walnut Street, 386–5679; 1800 Spring Garden Street, 567–2679; also in Abington, Plymouth Meeting, Malvern, Bala Cynwyd and Cherry Hill).

DANCE CLUB AFTER 2 A.M.: The **Black Banana** logo says it all, because there's no sign outside. Open till 3:30 every morning, once you've forked over the $55 membership fee, and famous—er, infamous—for those two-way bathroom mirrors (247 Race Street, 925–4433).

DINER, CITY: Call for an omelet and follow it up with the legendary sugar cookies at the landmark **Melrose Diner**. Quick service, snappy South Philly waitresses with elaborate coifs, classic diner menu and decor—one of the city's gems. Take an apple pie home to Mom—best wait 'till morning, though (1501 Snyder Avenue, 567–6644).

DINER, GREAT NORTHEAST: Have a club sandwich, read a tabloid and you'll be right at home at the always-open **Mayfair Diner and Dining Room**. They do takeout around the clock, too, in case you can't bear to change out of your pajamas (7373 Frankford Avenue, 624–8886).

FLOWER DELIVERY: There's no excuse to forget Mother's Day when you can dial **Flower World International** any time of the day or night to place an order. (The actual shop is open from 8 a.m. to 10 p.m.) All major credit cards are accepted (230 South Broad Street, 567–7100).

HOAGIE, CENTER CITY: Frankly, the most dependable latenighters are at **Wawa**—though of course it all depends on the commitment level of the hoagie crafter on duty that particular night (20th and Chestnut Streets, 751–0976; 15th and Locust Streets, and other locations).

HOAGIE, UNIVERSITY CITY: Exemplary waffle-cut fries, nifty neon clock and an admirable collection of Penn/Drexel memorabilia, but the real reason to get to **Abner's of University City** before 3 a.m. on weekends is the hoagie, a lifeboat of a sandwich whose essence drips seductively down to your elbows as you eat (3813 Chestnut Street, 662–0100).

HIP CAFE: Cafe Limbo caters to the Gen X crowd, but the food's genuinely fresh and good, and the prices even more palatable. Funky decor, tiny dance floor, pool table and lots of Keanu Reeves lookalikes. Dinner until 11 p.m. weekdays, 1 a.m. on weekends (2063 South Street, 545–8044).

MILKSHAKES: Add a grilled cheese and call it dinner, no matter what the clock is striking at Rittenhouse Square's **Diner on the Square**. All that neon makes everybody look weird at 3 a.m., but the place is usually packed (19th and Spruce Streets, 735–5787).

NEWSPAPERS: Your best bet for getting Sunday's *New York Times* at 11 p.m. Sunday: **Nite Owl News**. Leave the car engine running and make a quick getaway (Broad and Locust Streets).

PRESCRIPTIONS: Twenty-four-hour pharmacy service is a lifesaver of a convenience at the **Pathmark** on City Line Avenue (at Monument Avenue, Bala Cynwyd, 879-1292).

SANDWICHES AFTER MIDNIGHT: Oriental carpets cover the ceilings and stained glass gleams darkly, but **Chaucer's** is still a thoroughly unpretentious neighborhood bar where anyone can grab a booth or belly up to the bar for a beer and a huge veggie or tuna pita until 1:30 a.m. Above-average burgers, too (20th and Lombard Streets, 985–9663).

The Melrose Diner, a Philly classic 24 hours a day.

STEAMED CLAMS: For those special late-night cravings, **Sam's Clam Bar** serves corn on the cob, a dozen steamers for $6 and more atmosphere, frankly, than some folks can handle. Conveniently located between cheesesteak parlors Pat's and Geno's (Passyunk Avenue and 9th Street, no phone).

South Street Revisited

Just blocks away, horse-drawn carriages convey tourists through the serene, brick-paved streets where Ben Franklin trod in his silver-buckled shoes. But there is nothing quaint about South Street. Once immortalized in a rock-and-roll song as the "hippest street in town," it's a place where the smell of cheesesteaks casts an atmospheric veil over everything, and kids in search of excitement mingle with tourists gawking at the rude slogans on their T-shirts. South Street is a tarnished legend, once bohemian and now crassly commercial, but not without its own appeal.

ALTERNATIVE JAZZ JOINT: **Bob and Barbara's Lounge** may be the quintessential dive bar—cheap drinks, cheesy red vinyl decor, the ugliest light fixtures you've ever seen and a "hot table" serving chicken, biscuits and greens. With the Nate Wiley Quartet to back it all up, it doesn't get much funkier than this (1509 South Street, 545–4511).

BAR SCENE, FOR GROWNUPS: **Hurricane Alley**. Very tasty late-night snacks, big strong drinks and, for South Street, relatively mature patrons (328 South Street, 627–2803).

BODY PIERCING: Those with the urge get a simple hole in one ear, or opt for the lips, nose, tongue or various painful points south at **Infinity**. For what it's worth, they make a big deal about sanitary conditions (626 South Street, 923–7335).

HAPPY HOUR: Half a block south of South, **Xero** is a no-frills, loud-alternative-music dive with a convivial crowd and a weekend happy hour that sets just the right tone for hanging on South Street (613 South 4th Street, 619–0565).

STUFF: Discover contemporary jewelry, pottery, furniture and *objets*, all pricier and more fabulous than the "crafts" you'll find at the usual South Street storefront, at the **Works Gallery** (319 South Street, 922–7775).

THING SOUTH STREET HAS IN COMMON WITH MANAYUNK: A very hip store for feet of both sexes, **Benjamin Lovell Shoes** has a fleet of footwear, whether you're looking for ungainly Birkenstocks, fashionable fishermen's sandals or even the latest in creative recycling: shoes crafted from hemp. You know—*hemp* (318 South Street, 238–1969).

PLACE TO SHOP FOR DINNER: For Society Hill dwellers and anyone else lucky enough to be in the neighborhood, **Chef's Market** stocks everything a Julia Child fan or clever takeout artist could want to serve a meal with real panache. Great breads, too (231 South Street, 925–8360).

PLACE TO LINGER OVER CAPPUCCINO: **South Caffe**, with floor-to-ceiling windows that are open in the summer for Euro-style sidewalk cafe action. Hedonists get cappuccino *con panna* (with whipped cream) (627 South Street, 922–6454).

MUSIC VENUE: **Theater of the Living Arts**, otherwise known as **TLA** and not to be confused with the video rental store by the same name. You can catch acts from Dweezil Zappa's latest consortium to hippie holdovers like Richie Havens in this Haight-Ashbury-era theater (334 South Street, 922–1011).

GRUNGE BAR: You don't have to be Courtney Love to enjoy grubby **J.C. Dobbs**—though the Nirvana widow *did* repair here after the '94 Lollapalooza. You just have to be able to appreciate a good, old-fashioned, loud-music bar that's lasted longer than most establishments of its ilk (304 South Street, 925–4053).

CHEESESTEAK: You smell it wherever you go on South Street. The acrid, oniony scent clings to your clothes and your hair. So you may as well go ahead and just *eat* one already, in that black-and-white-tiled enclave of grease, Philly legend **Jim's Steaks** (400 South Street, 928–1911).

UNSUNG BOUTIQUE: Its dated name might suggest otherwise, but **Neo Deco** packs a lot of style for both sexes (414 South Street, 928–0627).

The Family Way:
Kids' Things to Do, See or Buy

Parents need all the help they can get when it comes to negotiating the straits of childhood for their young ones. Whether looking for educational exhibits, suitable shops, places for parties, or action-packed adventures, the area has everything a parent could want to plan any sort of activity.

Playtime

ADVICE: WHYY's **Dr. Dan Gottlieb**, psychologist and moderator of "Voices in the Family." Speak slowly and carry a big sensitivity.

ARCADE GAME RENTALS: Wouldn't a new, two-tier pinball machine with lights and music just *make* your preteen's next birthday party? **TNT Amusements**

rents all kinds of game machines, from foosball to Street Fighter, for all sorts of parties (1310 Industrial Boulevard, Southampton, 953–1188).

BIG-SCREEN MOVIES: Hold onto your hat at the **Tuttleman Omniverse Theater** at the **Franklin Institute**. Once the film begins, you'll feel as if you really are swooping down inside the Grand Canyon, scaling the Rockies and swimming right alongside the sharks (20th Street and the Benjamin Franklin Parkway, 448–1208).

BIRTHDAY PARTY FOR AGGRESSIVE KIDS: Provided you don't mind Junior brandishing a weapon—they shoot paint, but still—take him and his troop to **Gunnrunners**, a huge indoor paintball/skirmish game complex 20 minutes northwest of Cherry Hill (Beverly, NJ, 1–800–929–3719).

BIRTHDAY PARTY LOCATION: The **Philadelphia Zoo**. They're animals there already! The resident party planners have gained a reputation as experts in presenting Treehouse bashes for kids aged four to 11. Highlights include face-painting, comic skits about the environment and animal behavior, hot dogs, apple juice and ice cream. All you bring is the birthday cake—and the Tylenol (3400 West Girard Avenue, 243–1100).

BIRTHDAY PARTY ALTERNATIVE: **Recreation Station** is an indoor playground where kids can romp—safely, because the facility was designed to prevent major tumbles—through moonwalks, ball baths, slides, tubes and trapezes. It's *the* place to throw a child's birthday celebration on the Main Line (58 Greenfield Avenue, Ardmore, 610–645–5333).

BOOKSTORE: **Children's Book World** sponsors regular readings, storytelling programs and other incentives to get kids hooked on books and keep them there for life (17 Haverford Station Road, Haverford, 610–642–6247).

BOYS' CLOTHES: Most kids' shops treat a small guys' wardrobe as an afterthought; those smocked

dresses and flowered leggings are just so much more fun. Not the **Boy's Connection**, where lads are treated like sartorially astute men in training (286 Montgomery Avenue, Bala Cynwyd, 610–660–9330).

BURGER JOINT BELOVED BY KIDS: The atmosphere is crayon-bright at **Nifty Fifty's**, with fantastic swirls of neon and big red booths. The fare—malts, patty melts, burgers and other affable munchies—is irresistibly good. Try the filet mignon cheesesteak (1356 East Passyunk Avenue, 468–1950).

> Grab the gang and head to Nifty Fifty's, a diner with a twist.

CHILDREN'S SECTION IN A GROWNUP BOOKSTORE: The enthusiastic staff at **Encore Books** in King of Prussia can recommend kids' books because they've actually *read* them. Weekly book parties and story hours, a child-friendly layout and enormous selection make this a worthwhile stop near the big malls (DeKalb Plaza, 298–340 West DeKalb Pike, King of Prussia, 610–337–3393).

CLASSICAL MUSIC FOR CHILDREN: Send them to **Sound All Around Pre-School Concerts** (for preschool and kindergartners) and **Children's Concert Series** (with the Philadelphia Orchestra) at the Academy of Music. Now little Kristen can subscribe to her own series, and wave the baton along with Maestro Sawallisch (1420 Locust Street, 893-1946).

CLOTHES, GOOD-NATURED: There's a riotous funhouse of children's fashions at **Kamikaze Kids**, chosen by proprietors with their own passel of offspring to outfit (524 South 4th Street, 574–9800; Route 73, Marlton, NJ, 609–983–1100).

CLOTHES, DISCOUNT: Hartstrings is tidy and doesn't feel like an outlet, except where prices are concerned. Don't miss the twice-a-year progressive sale (821 Lancaster Avenue, Strafford, 610–971–9400).

COMEDY SHOWS: Comedy For Kids features hilarious fractured takes on classic plays, films and fairy tales. Occasional jokes fly right over the heads of the children—intentionally so, because the shows are brilliantly conceived to make adults laugh as much as the little ones (Actors Center Theater at the Bourse, 21 South 5th Street, 665–3996).

CRAFT STORE: **A.C. Moore** stocks enough unfinished wood toys and fingerpaints to keep kids creatively occupied until it's time to register for Art History 101 (2940 Springfield Road, Broomall, 610–353–1117).

EDUCATIONAL WORKSHOPS THAT ARE ACTUALLY FUN: Check the Saturday schedule of events at the **University of Pennsylvania Museum of Archaeology and Anthropology.** At each session, kids get to recreate the crafts of a different ancient or modern culture (33rd and Spruce Streets, 898–4000).

HAIRCUTS FOR CHILDREN: The *Aladdin* videos and animal chairs at **Kids Cuts** make trimming your little one's locks almost bearable (Routes 1 and 320, Springfield, 610–543–5006; 3203 Concord Pike, Wilmington, 302–479–0072).

HALLOWEEN MASKS: Deformed and hideous visages abound at **Wayne Toy Town.** Some of these ugly mugs are so big that they threaten to swallow up the child within (163 East Lancaster Avenue, Wayne, 610–688–2299).

LAYETTES: **The Children's Boutique** has tasteful fashions for newborns through preteens, with the emphasis on custom-designed layettes. Precious imported and handmade infant

An anaconda in the making in a craft workshop at the University of Pennsylvania Museum of Archaeology & Anthropology.

items abound, and the gift-wrapping is superb (1717 Walnut Street, 563–3881).

LOEHMANN'S FOR LITTLE ONES: The Children's Attic is a first-rate children's discount boutique, carrying all the latest styles and best names, at 40 to 80 percent off retail (262 South 19th Street, 985–2100).

NURSERY FURNISHINGS, GRAND: When no decorative flourish is too fabulous for your offspring, look over the wallpaper, accessories and cribs fit for a royal babe at **Bellini** (25 Cynwyd Road, Bala Cynwyd, 610–667–5177).

NURSERY FURNISHINGS, HUMBLE: The Scandinavian approach to babies' rooms—practical, bright and inviting—is reasonably priced and easy on design-conscious parents' eyes at **IKEA** (Plymouth Meeting Mall, Germantown Pike, Plymouth Meeting, 610–834–1520).

NURSERY PLANNERS: All thumbs design-wise? Call **The Baby's Room and the Kid's Room Too**. A representative will visit your home to draw up a plan, taking into consideration that you want your child to grow into the space in years to come (134 Bala Avenue, Bala Cynwyd, 610–664–2877; also in Frazer and Marlton, NJ).

PLACE FOR SINGLE PARENTS TO FLIRT WITH EACH OTHER WHILE THEIR KIDS PLAY IN THE SAND: Sunday afternoons in spring and summer, they head to **Maui** on the Delaware Avenue waterfront which features children's music, strolling minstrels and appropriate snacks for hungry little mouths (1143 North Delaware Avenue, 423–8116).

PLACE TO DRESS YOUR DAUGHTER LIKE ROYALTY: Beauteous girls' garments at **Her Royal Highness**—including stunning imports by Francoise Bouthillier—cost almost as much as Mom's clothes, but make a great impression (Suburban Square, 92 Coulter Avenue, Ardmore, 610–642–0456).

> # When the small fry get restless, it's time to go to the Philadelphia Zoo, the country's oldest zoo, and an innovator in animal conservation and breeding programs.

PLACE TO LET KIDS LEAVE THEIR GRUBBY LITTLE FINGERPRINTS: The **Please Touch Museum** is Philadelphia's most innovative institution for children seven and under. To describe the activities as merely hands-on would be an understatement, since kids are encouraged to "drive" a SEPTA bus and "rock-jump" till they drop (210 North 21st Street, 963–0667).

> You'll be climbing the walls when you visit the Garden State Discovery Museum.

PLEASE TOUCH MUSEUM ALTERNATIVE: The fledgling **Garden State Discovery Museum**, opened in 1994, is a modest but engaging educational funspot, with 15,000 square feet of discovery, imagination, and ten larger-than-life, hands-on exhibits. There are even special exhibits and fun

No grouches here... **Plunge into Sesame Place**.

workshops that explore Jersey classics, like The Discovery Diner, Down the Shore and the Nature Center. All for kids two to ten years old (16 North Springdale Road, 609–424–1233).

RADIO SHOW: Listen to thoughtful children call in to voice their opinions and asks questions on **WXPN's "Kid's Corner,"** weeknights at 7 p.m. at 88.5 on the FM dial. Like adult talk radio, it can become a daily addiction (898–6677).

STORE, OVERALL: **Zany Brainy**, the visionary books-and-games emporium, presents an ambitious schedule of free events—crafts workshops, "mini-concerts," book signings, movies, "Science Sundays" and much more of what makes being a smart kid so interesting (308 East Lancaster Avenue, Wynnewood, 610–896–1500; also in Strafford, Newtown, Jenkintown, Wilmington, DE and Moorestown, NJ).

TOY STORE: Trinkets, games, dolls and amusements for kids of all ages abound at **Einstein Books and Toys That Matter**. Ask for the shop's catalog, and be sure to check out the vast second floor full of fun-inducing merchandise (1627 Walnut Street, 665–3622).

UNDERRATED MUSEUM FOR DINOSAUR-MINDED KIDS: Take them to the **Academy of Natural Sciences** and avoid the teeming hordes down the street at the Franklin Institute. Let 'em loose in Dinosaur Hall instead (19th and the Benjamin Franklin Parkway, 299–1058).

UNIQUE BABY GIFTS: Those delicious, soft, handknit sweaters at **Born Yesterday**. Sure to be outgrown before they're outworn (1901 Walnut Street, 568–6556).

WATER PARK: Splash around at **Splash World**, a scream of a log-flume-and-then-some attraction at Clementon Amusement Park. With any luck, you'll catch one of the breathtaking dive demonstrations, too (Route 534/Clementon Blackwood Road, Clementon, NJ, 609–783–0263).

WATER SLIDES: The veritable smorgasbord of slippery options at **Sesame Place** includes some real thrillers for kids who have outgrown the Rubber Duckie Rapids, such as Sky Splash, a five-story water "adventure" (100 Sesame Road, Langhorne, 752–7070).

> Be sure to stop and smell the tulips—and dabble in the fountain—at Longwood Gardens.

WINTERTIME ACTIVITY FOR KIDS: The indoor Children's Garden at **Longwood Gardens** has curious mazes of plants and weird little secret fountains—all childscale, childproof and so appealing you'll wish you were small enough to participate (U.S. Route 1, Kennett Square, 610–388–6741).

Talking Shopping:
To Buy, Or Not to Buy

We've got swell-egant malls, discount centers and old-fashioned specialty stores to satisfy a passionate consumer or please the thriftiest tightwad. The whole area is a buyer's marketplace of options, from quirky to high-class.

....
Stores, Malls, Markets and More!

COWBOY BOOTS: Been looking for lizard in all the wrong places? Too bad, because **Southwest Style** has every pointy-toed style you could ever want (Plymouth Meeting Mall, 610–828–2833; also at Gateway Shopping Center, Valley Forge).

DEPARTMENT STORE: With its confectionary interior architecture and slightly faded elegance, the original branch of **John Wanamaker** (but please, we're on a lastname basis) remains Philadelphia's premier arena for big-store shopping. They'll even cook your Thanksgiving dinner (13th and Market Streets, 422–2000).

GAP: The one at 6th and South streets. Big and roomy; great sale area; and *shoes*, a remarkably hip selection, in fact (500 South Street, 627–7334).

IMITATION OF MADISON AVENUE: The block of Walnut Street that houses the city's two most exclusive men's clothiers, **Wayne Edwards** and **Allure** (1521 Walnut Street, 563–6801; 1509 Walnut Street, 561–4242).

LINGERIE, CITY: Victoria's Secret has its appeal, but for the finest in scanty European undies and nightclothes, climb the marble stairs to the tiny **Hope Chest**—it's quite the place on Valentine's Day (Shops at the Bellevue, Broad and Walnut Streets, 545–4515).

LINGERIE, 'BURBS: Silken teddies, charmeuse camisoles and slinky robes overflow the galore at **Marisha Fine Lingerie** (The Bridge at Foxcroft Square, Old York Road, Jenkintown, 887–7007).

LITTLE BLACK DRESSES: They can be clingy, swingy, loose, soft or bohemian, but they're *always* sexy. A dependable selection from the most fashion-forward designers is on the racks at **Knit Wit** (1721 Walnut Street, 564–4760; also at the Court at King of Prussia, Cherry Hill, Margate and Manayunk).

LUNCHTIME TREAT, NO CALORIES: A wander through mini-boutique **Plage Tahiti** might mean a silk soutache belt you didn't know you needed, or a pricey Bluefish ensemble. But it's a pause that refreshes (128 South 17th Street, 569–9139).

MALL, 'BURBS: The **Plaza** at King of Prussia just keeps on getting better with each expansion. You'll find that it's so all-consuming a shopping center, it's even worth

This stately eagle presides over Wanamakers Grand Court.

circumnavigating the frequent construction nearby to claim your rightful parking space (344 Mall Boulevard, King of Prussia, 610–337–1210).

MALL, CITY: Good things come in not-so-huge malls, judging by the nifty stores—including J. Crew, Country Roads Australia and Platypus—at Center City's **Shops at Liberty Place**, inside our flashy architectural statement, Liberty Place. The second-floor food court is an attraction all in itself (17th and Chestnut Streets, 851–9055).

> # Not so big that you'll get lost, and with some pleasant surprises amid its lineup of stores, the Shops at Liberty Place is definitely the best mall within the city limits.

MATERNITY CLOTHES: No floppy bows and virginal white collars at **Expecting One**—only real-life clothes for pregnant women, from classy designers like Tapemeasure and Japanese Weekend (115 Cynwyd Road at Bala Avenue, Bala Cynwyd, 610–668–1246).

MEN'S CLOTHIER, BIG SELECTION: With its grand old neoclassical building, three floors of traditional and hot new menswear and salesclerks who are nothing short of attentive, **Boyd's** is the best place in town for a man to decide just what suits him. Valet parking, too (1818 Chestnut Street, 564–9000).

Whirl around the world at Rand McNally in Liberty Place.

MOVE BY A STORE, CENTER CITY: Venerable Holt's Cigar Co. to the Deco-dently splendid Musselman's Pharmacy building on Walnut Street. Given the wild popularity of big-guy stogies, it's only fitting that this opulent spot features temperature-controlled private lockers for regular customers' private stock, a special smoking room with deep leather chairs and, we hope, a damn good fan (1522 Walnut Street, 732–8500).

Take your pick from a slew of items at J. Crew in Liberty Place.

MOVE BY A STORE, MAIN LINE: Danby Radio relocated from a cramped storefront on East Lancaster Avenue to state-of-the-art digs on West Lancaster. Don't let the modest name fool you; their high-tech audio-visual equipment rocks the music rooms of Main Line notables like Patti LaBelle (120 West Lancaster Avenue, Ardmore, 610–563–5686).

NEW SHOE THRILL: Aldo, the chock-full-of-styles shop whipping female browsers into a covetous, I-want-it-all frenzy in the Shops at Liberty Place (1625 Chestnut Street, 564–4630).

PETITES: Just because a woman has to stand on tiptoe to reach the top shelf doesn't mean she should have to wear childish clothes. That's what makes the sophisticated garb at La Petite Femme so special (Benjamin Fox Pavilion, Old York Road, Jenkintown, 885–6920; also in Haverford).

RESTAURANT IN A STORE, 'BURBS: A recent change of management has made hungry shoppers happy now that new owners have climbed aboard Le Train Bleu at Bloomingdale's

Manayunk:
Philly's Good-Times Neighborhood

Once a grimy industrial zone on the Schuylkill, Manayunk has been thoughtfully gentrified in recent years. Its back streets, winding up steep hills, are still full of modest two-family dwellings, but Main Street is now home to restaurants, bars, shops and galleries that lure savvy consumers from all parts of the city. A stroll along Main Street has become for adults the easygoing equivalent of a night on South Street for kids—browse, people-watch, have something amusing to eat and just sit back to enjoy the good life. To get there, take the Belmont Avenue/Green Lane exit off the Schuylkill Expressway (76W), cross the bridge and turn right at the light.

APPEARANCE BY A STORE: Dealing in women's glad rags like long, floaty dresses and crocheted sweaters—just the sort of ensemble one wears for a night out in Manayunk— **Ma Jolie** is housed in a spectacular old auto dealership building with ornate balconies, celestial clouds on the ceiling and innovative displays (4340 Main Street, 483–8850).

GALLERY: Whether it's gorgeous tree baubles at Christmas or tasteful handblown wine goblets, **Owen/Patrick Gallery** appeals

to the discriminating crafts shopper. Check out the oddly wonderful lighting fixtures (4345 Main Street, 482–9395).

Works of art at Owen/Patrick Gallery.

NEIGHBORHOOD CHINESE RESTAURANT: Actually, the low-key **Grasshopper** bills itself as "Sino-French," with elegantly unfettered food that combines the best of both worlds. Try chef Philip Tang's stellar salmon tartare with capers and caviar, and any of the dumplings (4427 Main Street, 483–1888).

NEIGHBORHOOD ITALIAN RESTAURANT: Expect richly sauced pastas, veal with panache and plenty of noise—whether you eat adjacent to the bar or upstairs in the quirky dining room—at convivial **Stephen's Restaurant and Bar** (105 Shurs Lane, 487–3136).

MEN'S CLOTHES: When it comes to loose, drapey sport shirts, interesting tie patterns and belts with cool buckles, it's a fine line between hip-enough-to-be-interesting and kinda-ridiculous-looking. And they do know the difference at bona fide guy's boutique **Pyramid** (4332 Main Street, 487–1788).

PLACE TO SPEND A RAINY SATURDAY: With 60 vendors exhibiting their trash-turned-treasures inside the **Manayunk Antique Flea Market**, the opportunities for stumbling upon something you adore are myriad (Main and Leverington Streets, 482–9004).

PLACE TO BUY A GIFT FOR A GUY WHO HAS EVERYTHING: Even *he* can't have every tie, boxer short and pair of socks by **Nicole Miller**, can he? The bright-eyed designer recently opened a shop dedicated to her unique creations (4249 Main Street, 930–0307).

(The Court at King of Prussia, 344 Mall Boulevard, 610–337–6300).

> A tantalizing feast for the eyes, as well as for the mouth, at Zagara's.

SENSE OF TIME: Second hands down, **Govberg Watches & Fine Jewelery** has the widest selection of the most coveted watches. Great if you can't make it to Geneva this year (1428 Walnut Street, 546–6505).

SERVICE IN A DEPARTMENT STORE: At downtown's **Strawbridge & Clothier**, the salesclerks have an old-fashioned sixth sense about what you need (8th and Market Streets, 629–6000; also in Exton, Echelon, Neshaminy, Plymouth Meeting, Cherry Hill, King of Prussia, Willow Grove and other regional malls).

SHOPPING CENTER, 'BURBS: The Main Line cultured club shops, including Laura Ashley, the Gap, Joan and David, their own genteel farmers' market and a score of other stores in timeless **Suburban Square** (between Lancaster and Montgomery Avenues, Ardmore, 610–896–7560).

SPECIALTY STORE: Sparkling mirrors, clouds of perfume, ultra-convenient parking and a swell selection of designer garb at **Saks Fifth Avenue**. Shopping here is a weekly ritual for the well-heeled women of Merion and beyond (City Line Avenue and Bala Cynwyd Place, Bala Cynwyd, 610–667–1550).

SUPERMARKET: And then some! **Zagara's** is a picture-perfect gourmet grocery, from each precisely placed organic apple to the luscious acreage of takeout foods behind gleaming glass cases. Even the macrobiotic stuff looks mouth-watering. And they sell paper towels, too (501 Route 73 South at Brick Road, Marlton, NJ, 609–983–5700).

SWIMSUITS: Shopping for bathing suits is a trying experience for women of all ages. That's why so many appreciate the personal attention at **Shirley & Co.**, where the sizes range from diminutive 5 to majestic 44. Any figure challenge you've got, they can fit (Huntingdon Valley Shopping Center, Huntingdon Pike, 663–8588; also in Cherry Hill).

WOMEN'S EVENING WEAR: The world is a-glitter inside **Beautiful Beads**, where sequins, spangles and bugle beads adorn elegant frocks for special occasions, from wedding days to big-nights-out (1921 Walnut Street, 567–4248).

WOMEN'S BOUTIQUE, CITY: Look-at-me jewelry, modish shoes and clothes, chatty salesclerks who would rather die than see you walk out empty-handed: the quintessential boutique, as defined by **asta de blue** (265 South 20th Street, 732–0550; also at Suburban Square, Ardmore).

WOMEN'S BOUTIQUE, SOUTH JERSEY: For she of discriminating eye and large wallet, who wants a salesclerk's full attention, **Florence Barufkin** carries sleek European career and evening clothes (295 West Marlton Pike, Cherry Hill, 609–429–9796).

WOMEN'S SHOES: There's fabulous footgear, including shoes that will change a person's look from nice to notorious, at **Mainly Shoes**. And what is style without a few pairs you can admire but wouldn't wear if your life depended on it? (4410 Main Street, Manayunk, 483–8000)

Cheap Chic:
Where the Bargains Are

ARMY SURPLUS: Their branch in Franklin Mills Mall can't hold a Sterno can to the original **Original I. Goldberg**'s great cheap blankets, duffel bags, vintage pajamas and who knows what else (902 Chestnut Street, 925–9393).

BARGAINS, GENERAL: Take your patience (those ancient elevators are *slow!*) and check your shopping bags at the door when you enter **Daffy's**. Dig through the dross for high-end, low-priced duds for children, men and especially for women (17th and Chestnut Streets, 963–9996).

BED LINENS, DISCOUNT: Whether you're feathering a new nest or just looking for ways to upgrade, there's a huge range of possibilities at **Bed, Bath & Beyond**. The "Beyond" refers to the kitchen (Franklin Mills Mall, 1455 Franklin Mills Circle at Woodhaven Road, 281–9266).

DESIGNER DISCOUNTS, UNEXPECTED: On sleepy Main Street in Hatboro, the **Sweater Mill** features everyday discounts of up to 50 percent off sportswear for men and women. It's a small space, but the selection is so well chosen, you're destined to buy (115 South York Road, Hatboro, 441–8966).

DISCOUNT SHOPPING EVENT: Fashion-forward Philadelphians await the coming of spring and the annual discount blowout of men's and women's jewelry, accessories and clothing, almost all from local designers and manufacturers, sponsored by the **Philadelphia Theater Company** (592–8333).

END-OF-SEASON SALE: Head for the venerable **Elegance by Edythe** in the Great Northeast, a vast compendium of women's and children's boutiques that's gobbled up a whole city block over the years. Bargains abound in June, for the store closes up for two months in summer, just like in the old days (6902–16 Bustleton Avenue, 624–5060).

FABRICS: For the best selection and prices in materials for clothing or interior decorating, you can't beat the shops on South 4th Street—in particular, **A. Brood & Sons** (727 South 4th, 925–0776) for drop-dead damasks, tapestries and brocades; **Marmelstein's** (9760 South 4th, 925–9862) for unusual trimmings; and **Kincus Fabrics** (755 South 4th, 923–8836) for dreamy bridal silks.

GOURMET BASICS: Assouline and Ting has ridiculously low prices on imported crackers, condiments, pastas and coffee beans, not to mention foie gras and Russian caviar. And don't worry, the neighborhood isn't as bad as it looks. Ask about the first-rate cooking classes taught by every accomplished restaurant chef in town (314 Brown Street, 627–3000).

HAUTE COUTURE OUTLET: The **First Choice** store in Franklin Mills is a tiny outlet run like a boutique. Gorgeous Mall Escada and Nic Janik ensembles—suits, black-tie dresses, leather jackets—are already marked down by half when they arrive here, then reduced another half toward the end of the season (1455 Franklin Mills Circle at Woodhaven Road, 281–3966).

HOUSEPLANTS, CHEAP: Home **Depot**, believe it or not, which will pot them for free if you buy one of the nice terra-cotta or hand-painted planters. They also guarantee all foliage for a year (1601 South Columbus Boulevard, 218–0600; also in Mount Laurel, Lawnside, Bensalem, Montgomeryville and Willow Grove).

Choices galore, at Dan's Cancellation Shoes.

MEN'S BARGAIN SHOES: Clever gentlemen pick up their Bruno Maglis and other fabulous footwear for a pittance at the **Neiman-Marcus Outlet** in Franklin Mills Mall (1887 Franklin Mills Circle, 637–5900).

MEN'S CLOTHES, DISCOUNT: For those who tend toward the traditional, **Thos. David** is the place to search out khakis, rep ties and nice gray suits (Fourth and Race Streets, 922–4659; also in Haverford, East Falls and Northeast Philadelphia).

WOMEN'S CLOTHES, DISCOUNT: There are Loehmann's, and then there are **Loehmann's**. The best are the North Jersey originals, and Cherry Hill's will do in a pinch, but the enormous **Drexel Hill** branch beats them all, bejeweled hands down (1053 Pontiac Road, 610–789–9100).

WOMEN'S SHOES, DISCOUNT: Salesmen calling out, "Ladies, who needs a mate?" combined with a range of cheap-to-costly footwear displayed on crammed racks makes for a unique Philly experience at **Dan's Cancellation Shoes** (1733 Chestnut Street, 568–5257).

Books and Music

AFFORDABLE LIMITED-EDITION BOOKS AND ARTWORK: Many literarily inclined Philadelphians shop at the **Print Club**, a great source of high-minded gifts for the hard-to-buy-for (1614 Latimer Street, 735–6090).

BOOKSTORE: It's difficult to imagine what Center City was like before **Borders Book Shop & Espresso Bar** came to town. A whole lifestyle of a store, with helpful salesclerks, great cappuccino, magazines and chairs for browsing away a rainy day (1727 Walnut Street, 568–7400; also in Rosemont and Marlton, NJ).

BOOKSTORE, LUXURIOUS: You feel like hot stuff just walking into the posh and spacious **Rizzoli** inside the Shops at the Bellevue. Along with the books, charming frames, stationery and gifts are a few aesthetically superior T-shirts (Broad and Walnut Streets, 546–9200).

BOOKSTORE, POLITICALLY INCLINED: **House of Our Own**, with lots of new and used volumes from small and university presses. Contemporary cultural and social issues are the specialty (3920 Spruce Street, 222–1576).

BOOKSTORE, SUBVERSIVE: **Wooden Shoe Books & Records**, reeking of incense, is the place to find Emma Goldman's diaries, *The Anarchist Cookbook* and lots of very impolite comic books (112 South 20th Street, 569–2477).

CDs, POPULAR: Don't bat an eye if you see uniformed security guards escorting a handcuffed petty thief out of **Tower Records**— the deafening, multi-storied South Street branch of this chain has so many discs in stock, it must be tempting (610 South Street, 574–9888; 9173 Roosevelt Blvd., 676–1578).

> Come marvel at the selection at Fat Jack's Comicrypt.

CDs, CLASSICAL: Tower Records' classics branch on South Street may have a wider selection, but modest **Muchnik's** has knowledgeable salespeople who know and love music—and can offer heartfelt opinions to help you choose the best recordings (1725 Sansom Street, 564–0209).

COMIC BOOKS: Not for boys only, judging by the number of grown men in suits flipping through the latest superhero mags

Open for early-morning coffee and after-dinner browsing, Borders Book Shop & Espresso Bar has brought a new way of life to downtown Walnut Street, once known mainly for its bustle during business hours.

at lunchtime in **Fat Jack's Comicrypt** (2006 Sansom Street, 963–0788; also in Olney, Overbrook Park and Oaklyn, NJ).

DULCIMERS: Folks into folk harps and folksy recordings flock to the **Flop-Eared Muse** (759 South 4th Street, 923–0273).

HIGH-END STEREO STORE, CITY: Sleek, spare showrooms where design-conscious components are displayed like fine *objets* in a contemporary art museum, and very attentive service—that's **David Mann Audio** (NewMarket, 2nd and Lombard Streets, 922–3000).

HIGH-END STEREO STORE, 'BURBS: Soundex, for custom installation and quality components. You'll also find a good selection of pre-owned equipment that's easy on the budget (1100 Easton Road, Willow Grove, 659–8815).

HOME THEATER EQUIPMENT: HiFi House, with wholesale prices on equipment for that media room you've been meaning to install in the basement (1001 Sussex Boulevard, Broomall, 544–4420).

LASER DISC RENTAL: If you've gone out and bought the darn machine, you may as well see everything that's available for viewing on it, and the best place to go is Blockbuster Video (534 South Street, 928–9600).

MAGAZINE SELECTION, HIGH-MINDED: Get your *Donna Moda* and Dunhill cigarettes at Avril 50. But please, park your dripping wet umbrella at the door (3406 Sansom Street, 222–6108).

MAGAZINE SELECTION, OVERALL: Tower Books, as civilized as Tower Records is wild, has a vast rack with French and Italian *Vogue*s, every homemade fanzine imaginable and whole sections given over to tattooing, body piercing and other acute pursuits (425 South Street, 925–9909).

MUSIC LOVERS' GIFTS: Hit Intermission in Chestnut Hill for original Broadway musical posters, rare jazz CDs, scores to shows you never heard of, books and memorabilia galore (8405 Germantown Avenue, 242–8515).

PLACE TO BUY COOKBOOKS: In about 12 square feet of space, the Cookbook Stall at Reading Terminal Market has hundreds of titles, from Pennsylvania Dutch specialties to exotic Indonesian fare (12th and Arch Streets, 923–3170).

PLACE TO TRADE IN USED CDs: This particular branch of the Philadelphia Record Exchange is also the best place to buy those old-fashioned vinyl LPs (608 South 5th Street, 925–7892).

RECORDS, JAZZ: The extensive selection of jazz and R&B at Third Street Jazz and Rock. They also carry tapes, and aficionados can come to read the album covers for hours (20 North Third Street, 627–3366).

RECORDS, USED: Pretty soon all records will be used goods, but for now the best general selection of secondhand LPs in first-hand condition can be found at Plastic Fantastic Record Exchange (26 West Lancaster Avenue, Ardmore, 610–896–7625).

VIDEO RENTAL: TLA, with qualifications, because the clerks are rude, and there's no dropoff slot for movie returns. But the selection and organization are superior (517 South 4th Street, 922–3838; 1808 Spring Garden Street, 751–1171; 1520 Locust Street, 735–7887).

Wedding Day Dos

BRIDAL REGISTRY: **The China Collection.** They'll tactfully distract the mom while giving the bride-to-be an honest opinion. (But Mom, as is her wont, is usually right.) The recent expansion affords plenty of room to decide (31 East Wynnewood Road, Wynnewood, 610–649–0850).

BRIDAL REGISTRY FOR YOUNG COUPLES: Utterly tasteful crystal and china at **Tiffany & Co.**—and if you have all you need, you can always spend the rest on diamonds (1414 Walnut Street, 735–1919).

BRIDAL REGISTRY FOR SOPHISTICATES: **Fante's.** Because *nobody* owns all the coffee paraphernalia and French copper pots they really want, no matter how many times they've been married. They discount, too—tell your relatives (1006 South 9th Street, 922–5557; also in Springfield, King of Prussia and Exton Square).

BRIDAL REGISTRY, SECOND MARRIAGE: **Table of Contents** in Suburban Square. Since you already have everything you need, here's where to find everything you want (27 on the Square, 610–645–9559).

Gowns fit for a bride at Suky Rosan.

BRIDAL VEIL DESIGN: Cheryl Connor of **Peg Connor Couturiere** can take one look at a gown and come up with just the right topping: an insouciant pouf of tulle, a simple damask headband or something in between (1530 Locust Street, 985–2173).

GOWNS: Many well-heeled Philly brides have stood atop the platform in a mirrored chamber and been fussed over, fitted and outfitted by the indomitable **Suky Rosan**. Her posh salon also carries important frocks for other momentous occasions (4953 Anderson Avenue, Suburban Square, Ardmore, 610–649–3686; Shops in the Bellevue, Broad and Walnut Streets).

GOWNS, ALTERNATIVE: At small and chic **Sophy Curson**, imports from France and England are flourished before the bride-to-be. The service is impeccable. For other events, perhaps Curson can pull out a Jean Muir or a flashy Christian Lacroix that will do (19th and Sansom Streets, 567–4662).

PLACE TO COMPLETE YOUR PATTERN: China Outlet and Gourmet Garage—two great big bargain outlets for tableware, linens and housewares. The humongous napkin section alone can send an indecisive person into paroxysms of panic (993 Route 73 South, Marlton, NJ 609–988–0333; 443 Shore Road, Somers Point, NJ 609–927–5299).

SCOUTING MISSION FOR BRIDES AND THEIR MOTHERS: A trip to famed Bucks County wedding-gown discounter **Anne Bailey's**. Even if you get your frock here (and many do), you never admit it (Route 313 at Ferry Road, Fountainville, 345–8133).

SHOES: Step into delicious, creamy brocade mules and beaded slippers with elegant small heels at **Toby Lerner**, the fashionable clothing-shoe-jewelry boutique patronized by Philly women too fabulous to shop around for bargains (117 South 17th Street, 568–5760; also in Suburban Square, Ardmore).

WEDDING CAKES: Roslyn House Cakes, created by Bradley High. He greets prospective clients at Roslyn House, Quaker architect William Price's replica of a Scottish castle, and is likely to suggest grown-on-the-premises gooseberries as a filling. By appointment only, my dear (500 Oakley Road, Haverford, 610–649–7341).

WEDDING GIFTS, HIP: Start them out with a new-classic Nambe' bowl, a couple of exquisite brocade pillows or something gilt and luxurious at **Urban Objects**. Great gift boxes, too (1724 Sansom Street, 557–9474).

WEDDING GIFTS, TRADITIONAL: An old Philly jeweler in a grand Beaux Arts building designed by famed architect Horace Trumbauer, **J.E. Caldwell** goes far beyond baubles to all the niceties a couple wants for their new life, from classic Waterford to stylish Rosenthal china (Chestnut and Juniper Streets, 864–7800; also in Chestnut Hill, Haverford and King of Prussia).

The Stuff of Life

ANTIQUES TREND-SETTER: Every April, the **Philadelphia Antiques Show**—one of the most important of such events in the country—brings together eminent exhibitors of American and English art and furniture. If Adirondack is the theme, expect prices in Adirondack furniture to soar (387–3500).

ASIAN TREASURES: Michelle Liao's **Liao Collections** has Chinese and Japanese antiques, from screens to teapots, buddhas to bed frames. If you're not a famous client like David Byrne or Kurt Vonnegut, check it out anyway—especially that bilingual parrot in the window, who curses in Taiwanese (607–609 Bainbridge Street, 925–1809).

AUCTION: **Freeman Fine Arts.** Leave a written bid on that settee in the giant, two-story salesroom, or ogle at the paintings, china, furniture and decorative miscellany. Auctions are Wednesdays at 10 a.m. (1808 Chestnut Street, 563–9275).

BED LINENS: The finest Frette sheets—we're talking *real linen* here—plus plush damasks and kitten-soft throws at **Maleka Fine Linens** (Suburban Square, Ardmore, 610–896–7181).

BICYCLES, 'BURBS: Philly and environs offer several good choices, but for price-plus-service on top-name street and mountain bikes and accessories, **Performance Bicycle Shop** outpedals the pack (1776 East Lancaster Avenue, Paoli, 610–644–8522; also in North Wales and Huntingdon Valley).

CLASSIC CAR KITS: Build yourself a 427 S/C Cobra for tooling the country roads on weekends, or spring for a Mirage ski and fishing boat at **Royal Motorsport & Marine** (99 North Caln Road, Coatesville, 610–384–5709).

CHRISTMAS ORNAMENTS: Of all places, the design-conscious **AIA Bookstore**, owned and operated by the Philadelphia Chapter of the American Institute of Architects. From exquisite miniature cherubim to fanciful little Windsor chairs, your tree won't look like anyone else's (117 South 17th Street, 569–3188).

CIGARS: As cigar smoking has grown in popularity, the walk-in humidor room at **Holt's Cigar Co.** has gotten more crowded with Philly's power puffers, but the service is as casually solicitous as ever. It's *the* place to pick up a box of stately Romeo Y Julietas, a fat Waterman fountain pen, a gorgeous burled humidor—all the status props for the successful man (1522 Walnut Street, 732–8500).

FABULOUS LIGHT FIXTURES: A bright selection of antique and vintage pieces at **Classic Lighting Emporium**, including that Manny, Moe and Jack light you've been looking for. They can repair any old torchiere or sconce too (62 North 2nd Street, 625–9552).

FLOWER VENDOR: Sunflowers, lilacs and other less-hackneyed buds bloom among the baby's breath at the cart at the corner of 17th and Walnut Streets.

GARDEN FURNISHINGS: Martha Stewart fell in love with Brian Foster's rustic-chic trellises and other accoutrements of the leafy life, available through Foster's **Garden Architecture** catalog (719 South 17th Street, 545–5442).

GARDEN SHOP, CITY: Pick up organic fertilizer and pesticide along with terra-cotta pots, perennials and herbs at **Green Acres** (263 South 10th Street, 238–1810).

GARDEN SHOP, 'BURBS: **Waterloo Gardens** is a leafy green world in itself: perennials, shrubs, bulbs, fertilizers, furnishings and plenty of good advice from the huge, well-trained staff (136 Lancaster Avenue, Devon, 610–293–0800; 200 North Whitford Road, Exton, 610–363–0800).

GIFTS FOR CAR BUFFS: **Car Crazy** has detailing products, automotive artwork and even key rings for that old TR6 collecting cobwebs in the garage (723 Montgomery Avenue, Narberth, 610–667–4333).

GREETING CARDS: Assuming you're not in the market for cards displaying naked butts of either sex (in which case South Street has no peer), the grunge-chic department store, **Urban Outfitters,** has a wallful of treasures (4040 Locust Street, 387–0373; 1809 Walnut Street, 564–2313).

HARDWARE STORE, CITY: **National Hardware**, right off Spring Garden. The only antidote to a world gone mad at Home Depot (462 North 4th Street, 627–1091).

HARDWARE STORE, 'BURBS: **True Value Hardware** has custom window shades, popsicle trays for your freezer, Interplak toothbrushes—this is hardware we *like*. And the prices are truly discounted (205 West Lancaster Avenue, Wayne 610–293–1777).

LUGGAGE: There's always a price break and lots of stock on hand at **Robinson's**. It's *the* place to replace your threadbare garment bag with a sleek and practically indestructible Tumi bag (Broad and Walnut Streets, 735–9859; also in Cherry Hill, Ardmore, Jenkintown and Chadds Ford).

NURSERY: No rakes, wreaths, potting soil or seeds, just tasteful and unusual perennials at **Renny the Perennial Farm**, owned by legendary Manhattan society florist Renny Reynolds. It's worth the drive to central Bucks County some balmy spring day for watercolor-soft primroses and other exclusive blooms (Brown's Mills Road, Wrightstown, 598–0550).

PATIO FURNITURE: When price is no object, get your new Brown Jordan suite and plenty of deferential attention at **William Frederick**

Patio Furniture 8705 Germantown Avenue, Chestnut Hill, 247–1668; also in Montgomeryville, Bryn Mawr and Avalon, NJ).

POLITICALLY CORRECT STORE: A vague category, perhaps, but you'll understand once you've experienced **Anthropologie**, with its elegant-earthy furniture, bedding, men's and women's clothes, jewelry, tablesettings, books and gardening accoutrements.

Beds, linens and other earthy furnishings at Anthropologie.

It's a seductive oasis for pursuers of the natural-fiber life (201 West Lancaster Avenue, Wayne, 610–687–4141).

POOCH PARLOR: **Lick Your Chops**, a veritable feast for the four-legged set, with gourmet dog biscuits and bird cookies fresh from the in-store bakery (700 North Second Street Pike, Richboro, 322–5266).

SAILING GEAR: First-rate for first mates and captains, **Sail Gear** carries a seaworthy selection of rigging, hardware, instruments, books, binoculars and nautical gifts (The Chestnut Village Shoppes, Chestnut Road, Paoli, 610–408–9260).

SEX AIDS: Not that you need them, of course. But should a visit to an erotic emporium be the order of the day, you may as well skulk into one in a respectable neighborhood: **The Pleasure Chest** (2039 Walnut Street, 561–7480).

SOFAS, HIGH-END: Sure, you could buy a new car. But you could also spend the money on a buttery-soft, low-slung showpiece of a couch from **Roche Bobois**, and lounge in luxury for the rest of your days. Hook up with a decorator or call for an appointment (Marketplace Design Center, 2400 Market Street, 972–0168).

SOFAS, EVERYDAY: The populist Swedish-born superstore **IKEA** has come a long way in the seating department. With custom upholstery and sturdy construction, its sofas are a great value—and they range from floral traditionals to that icy, retro-Danish-modern look (Plymouth Meeting Mall, Germantown Pike, Plymouth Meeting, 610–834–1520).

SOFAS, LEATHER: There's a different feeling when you shop at a family-owned-and-operated establishment like the **Leather Furniture Shops**. By the time you leave, you'll have seen about 300 styles and you'll know more about grades of leather and dyeing processes than you ever dreamed was possible (31 North 2nd Street, 592–1440).

SPORTING GOODS, CITY: Two floors of bright athletic merchandise for virtually every popular sport, from basketball to blading, plus all the current sneaker manifestations at **Herman's** (1708 Chestnut Street, 335–7660).

SPORTING GOODS, 'BURBS: Get your racquets restrung, outfit yourself for a jaunt to Aspen Mountain or buy Mom a new nine iron at classy emporium **Danziesen and Quigley** (Route 70 at 295, Cherry Hill, NJ, 609–424–5969).

Travel along Lancaster Avenue from Bryn Mawr to Devon, making sure to stop in at Borders, Zany Brainy, Anthropologie and Fresh Fields on the way! By the time you pull over for geraniums at Waterloo Gardens, you'll be broke—but satisfied.

TRAVEL STORE: **Traveler's Emporium** has everything for your sojourn, from the perfect suitcase and nifty travel appliances to obscure plugs for those Fourth World outlets. Even if you're not planning a trip, check out the selection of handsome urban backpacks (210 South 17th Street, 546–2021).

WALLPAPER: **Colonial Wallcoverings** has gorgeous, pricey reproduction papers by master designers, including Frank Lloyd Wright and the British Arts and Crafts pioneer William Morris. They're just the thing with your Stickley armchair (707 East Passyunk Avenue, 351–9300).

Old City:
Positively Third Street

Cross lower Manhattan's hipper-than-any-thing SoHo district with Philadelphia's historic quarter of warehouses and artists' lofts, and you get Old City. This eight-block enclave of art galleries and showrooms of fine art, antiques, furniture and decorative objects on and off North Third Street is one of Philly's most intriguing neighborhoods.

CHAIRS: Butt of course—at stylish **Jasuta Urban Interiors**, every-thing from Porsche anodized aluminum stacking chairs to estate-sale settees (122–124 Arch Street, 627–6670).

GALLERY FOR CRAFTS LOVERS: The superior arts and crafts showplace **Snyderman Gallery**, which pulled up roots on South Street when it became clear that Old City was the next hip place to be. Now, in a majestic space on a tiny side street, it's a trove of handsome glass, pottery and sculpture by some of the nation's premier craftspeople (303 Cherry Street, 238–9576).

HANGOUT: Peruse a British newspaper, browse through the used books, challenge someone to a chess game or scribble a poem on the complementary notepad at **Quarry Street Cafe**. The coffee's dark and rich, and refills are just 50 cents (147 North 3rd Street, 413–1360).

PARTY: The lively action on **First Fridays**—the first Friday evening of every month (except for July and August), when Philadelphia's art lovers and bohemian poseurs wander through Old City munching cheese cubes, sipping from paper cups of wine and browsing through galleries that keep late hours for the occasion.

FIRST FRIDAY ITINERARY: Okay, here's the drill: Park on 3rd Street by 6 p.m. Nip into **olc**, the **Philadelphia Furniture League**, **Snyderman Gallery** and **Moderne**. Cut down Church Street. By 7:30, you've hit the **Clay Studio**, **Zone One** and **F.A.N.** galleries. At 9 p.m. sharp, you're at **Sugar Mom's Church Street Lounge** sipping a margarita with the rest of the cool folks.

ITALIAN HOME FURNISHINGS: You'll find the very tip of the cutting edge at **olc**, a rigorously ascetic gallery of imported lighting fixtures and furniture. Cats posing languidly atop the sleek merchandise add a certain cachet (152–154 North 3rd Street, 923–6058).

ANIMATION CELS: Whether your tastes run to *The Lion King* or *Snow White*, you'll find Walt Disney Studios hand-painted cels in limited editions at **Animation Art Resources** (118 North Third Street, 925–2009).

FURNISHINGS BY PHILADELPHIA ARTISANS: The **Philadelphia Furniture League** is a cooperative gallery space of furniture and decorative accessories by respected creators like Jack Larimore, Bob Ingram and Liz Galbraith. It's just the place to find a lamp, sofa or dining table unlike any other (160 North 3rd Street, 440–7136).

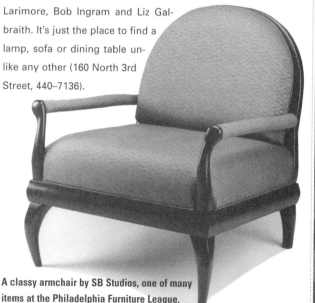

A classy armchair by SB Studios, one of many items at the Philadelphia Furniture League.

At Your Service:
How to Get Things Done

AIRPORT LIMO: Whether you require a white stretch limo (tacky, tacky!), a sedate sedan or a mini-van to fetch or drop off a claque of out-of-town colleagues, trust **Philadelphia Airport Shuttle & Kiwi Express**—seen all over Center City, depositing important people at important places (969–1818).

ALL-PURPOSE REPAIRS: **Wanamakers** will clean and restuff pillows, repair electric shavers and luggage, rebind blankets and monogram almost anything your ego desires (13th and Market Streets, third floor mezzanine, 422–2331).

ANGELS: The volunteers at **Manna** conjure up 11,000 balanced, beautifully presented meals a month—ginger chicken and risotto, double-chocolate mousse cake—and deliver them to homebound people with AIDS. They also serve as a daily support system, helping to keep body and soul together (486–2662).

ANTIQUE FURNITURE REUPHOLSTERY: A. Cocco and Sons restored George Washington's French armchair for the Historical Society of Pennsylvania. Reupholstering, restoration and custom reproductions are their specialties, and though most of the work comes from decorators, they'll welcome you, too (2320 Grays Ferry Avenue, 545–6693).

BOOKBINDING: During her internship in the rare books conservation department at the Library of Congress and while training at Harvard University, **Nancy Nitzberg** worked on volumes dating to the fifteenth century. She's an expert in the structural problems of antique bindings (Washington Lane, Jenkintown, 886–3460).

BOOKS ON TAPE RENTAL: Opt for a motivational work, or tune into Michael Crichton's latest at **Listen Up Audio Books**. If time allows, sip a cappuccino and sample some tapes before deciding (1507 Chestnut Street, 568–7255).

BOOK DELIVERY: Read a review that makes you want to crack open that new novel *now*, then pick up the phone and dial **Robin's Book Store**, where "knowledgeable human beings assisted by modern technology" help bring it on home to you (108 South 13th Street, 1–800–BOOKS–38).

CHEESESTEAK DELIVERY: Many have tried, but few can beat **A Taste of Philadelphia**'s well-organized overnight delivery of hoagies, cheesesteaks and other fine examples of our indigenous cuisine (800–846–2443).

CHINA RESTORATION: Pick up the pieces of that smashed Limoges tureen and carry them over to **Harry A. Eberhardt China and Porcelain**, a cluttered shop which claims to be the country's oldest and largest restorer of china, porcelain and crystal (2010 Walnut Street, 568–4144).

CLASSIC LIMOUSINE RENTAL: Impress your friends. Heck—impress *yourself* by having a chauffered Rolls-Royce Silver Cloud drive you around for a special evening. Call **Classic Cars** (877–8048).

DAY SPA, CITY: Check into **Pierre & Carlo**, and check out hours later looking like a sleek new man or woman. Facilities at this Roman-style spa are spotlessly clean and utterly private, and the staff's just friendly enough (Fountain Court, Shops at the Bellevue, Broad and Walnut Streets, 790–9910).

DAY SPA, 'BURBS: Spa BiBa is a wildly luxurious salon in the posh Bridge at Foxcroft Square mall. Get a quick haircut and massage, or go for the total queen-for-a-day treatment (Old York Road, Jenkintown, 572–7444).

DELIVERY SERVICE FOR URBAN AGORAPHOBIC COMPULSIVES: Call up and demand beer—from swell microbrews to pedestrian "industrials"—plus cigarettes, snacks, ice and fruit juice for the morning after from **Franklin Beer Distributors** (1837 Callowhill Street, 557–8643).

DOG WALKING: Bonded animal lovers from **Chambley & Co.** will take Spike out for a stroll or just feed and visit her while you're away from home (545–6730).

EYEBROWS: For those who care—and some do, especially once they've seen the difference a change can make in their overall appearance—Rosemary Beauchemin at the **Beau Institute** wreaks magic on shapeless brows (2020 Locust Street, 893–1133).

Elegant arrangements of all styles, at Thoughts in Bloom.

FACIALS, CITY: The **Body Klinic** is the next wave in skin care for both sexes. The hip, young, knowledgeable staff uses pure, natural ingredients in all their facials, massages and more esoteric treatments (2012 Walnut Street, 563–8888).

FACIALS, MAIN LINE: Ilona Csaky at **Ilona Bio-Aesthetics** is a *fanatic* about skin quality, and has the dewy countenance to back up her beliefs. She studied extensively in her native Hungary, where gorgeous skin is second nature. Surrender your pores to her firm fingertips (411 East Lancaster Avenue, Wayne, 610–687–4444).

FLORIST, CITY: Thoughts in Bloom, just off Rittenhouse Square, doesn't carry any dud buds. The wrapping is as delicious as the flowers themselves (18th and Locust Streets, 732–1100).

FLORIST, SUBURBS: Fresh, on time and handsomely arranged: that's the dependable result from venerable **Robertson's Florists** (850 Germantown Avenue, Chestnut Hill, 242–6000).

FLOWER DELIVERY, MAIN LINE: Tasteful enough to woo Martha Stewart, by the folks at **Flowers And** ... in Haverford Square. They buy many blooms locally, so arrangements stay fresher, have truer colors and smell the way they should (385 West Lancaster Avenue, Haverford, 1–800–Garden9).

FRAMING, CUSTOM: Ursula Hobson Fine Art Framing has all the utterly tasteful components, from matte boards to gorgeous, exotic frames. She also carries the city's finest selection of antique prints (1602 Pine Street, 546–7889).

FRAMING, DO-IT-YOURSELF: Despite that box of sharp tools and lethal-looking nails, it's not so difficult to frame your own prints and photos at **Framers**

Workroom—especially with employees so focused and ready to lend a hand (2103 Walnut Street, 567–6800; also in Jenkintown and Cherry Hill, NJ).

FUR COAT REMODELING: Maybe you want it turned into a politically correct raincoat lining, or snipped into a fanciful jacket. Visit **Tarnopol Furs**, where a resident tailor does all work on the premises. They do expert cleaning of furs and leathers, too (345 Montgomery Avenue, Bala Cynwyd, 610–667–5444).

GIFT BASKETS: Basketfulls and More. Stuffed with buttery homemade *rugelach* and other cookies, plus snacks and munchies so seductive, you should probably send one to yourself (phone orders only: 677–6688).

HARDWARE MAINTENANCE AND REPRODUCTION: Whether you need your andirons straightened or your door hinges duplicated, take them to **Ball and Ball**. And while you're there, tour the surprising little museum of antique furniture and artifacts (463 West Lincoln Highway, Exton, 610–363–7330).

HEALTH CLUB, CITY: You'll definitely find better prices elsewhere, but you get what you pay for at the **Sporting Club**. It's a multi-level extravaganza, designed by architect superhero Michael Graves, with well-maintained equipment and spotless facilities. You also get the chance to see every city bigshot break a sweat (Hotel Atop the Bellevue, Broad and Walnut Streets, 985–9876).

HEALTH CLUB, SUBURBS: The machines in a busy gym get a bruising workout. All the more reason to laud the management of **Main Line Health and Fitness** for its assiduous attention to the maintenance of all the equipment, and for the scrupulous, almost-constant cleaning up after sweaty bods (931 Haverford Road, Bryn Mawr, 610–527–2200).

GUITAR RESTRINGING: Haul your twangy axe over the bridge to **Zapf's Music of Pennsauken**. On the other hand, shouldn't a musical legend-in-the-making be able to do it herself? (5811 Crescent Boulevard, Pennsauken, NJ, 609–488–4333).

HAT REPAIRS: **Wanamakers** is head and shoulders above the rest of the city in hat repairs. They'll reconstruct chapeaux for men or women in felt, velvet and straw, as well as replace linings, bands and accoutrements on anything from top hats to boaters (13th and Market Streets, third floor mezzanine, 422–2331).

LINGERIE, CUSTOM: For old-lady girdles or sweet-young-thing bustiers, no one surpasses the careful handiwork of seamstresses at the **Jay Ann Corset Shop**, deep in the heart of Northeast Philly (9331 Krewstown Road, 676–6191).

LOCKSMITH: For those inevitably embarrassing and potentially dangerous situations, find a phone and call **Houdini Lock & Safe**. It's open 24 hours—thank goodness (616 South Broad Street, 333–LOCK).

LONG-STEMMED ROSES: **RosExpress** edges out the others for super-tall roses that always arrive fresh and dewy, always bloom large and always last at least a week, even if you're mean to them (351–0100).

MAKEUP CONSULTATION: By appointment only, at the sleek and stylish **Raya-Haig** salon in Bala Cynwyd. The eavesdropping alone is worth the cost of the consultation (401 City Avenue, 610–668–5373).

MARBLE REFINISHING: **European Marble Floor Refinishing** restores and maintains all marble, slate, granite and terrazzo surfaces. Proper stone care at last (860–9111).

> **Treat yourself to a luxurious lunch-break at Toppers Spa.**

MASSAGE, CITY: By any of the strong, seasoned hands at **Toppers Spa**, a clean, tranquil getaway in the midst of the city (Rittenhouse Hotel, Rittenhouse Square, 546–1850; also at the Bourse, 21 South 5th Street, 627–3545 and in Voorhees, NJ).

MASSAGE, SUBURBS: Man or woman, mildly stressed or a bundle of nerves—off you go to **Pastore Hair Salon & Day Spa** (570 West DeKalb Pike, Suite 2, King of Prussia, 610–337–2044).

MOVERS: **A Little Help Inc.** is not your ordinary bunch of burly bruisers. They handle moves involving fine furniture, artworks and antiques, and are skilled in the art of assembling and dismantling large, important pieces of furniture (739–2742).

ORCHIDS: Gentlemen, roses may get you noticed, but orchids from **Trillium** will get you a lot farther than that (342 Righters Mill Road, Gladwyne, 610–642–8140).

Need your pooch exercised or your book bound? Nearly every little service and detail is available—at a price, of course.

ORIENTAL RUG REWEAVING: There's free pickup and delivery for reweaving done on the premises by skilled restorers at **Paulsons and Co. Oriental Rugs** (100 Park Avenue, Swarthmore, 610–543–6000).

PIANO TUNING: **Jacob's Music** services the Philadelphia Orchestra and the Mann Music Center. Need we say more? (1718 Chestnut Street, 568–7800).

PLACE TO GET ANYTHING AIRBRUSHED: The **Airbrush Place**. Aficionados think nothing of paying $70 to have their faces airbrushed on a T-shirt here. They also did the walls at the Iguana Club, Cafe Limbo and Mako's (1830 East Passyunk Avenue, 463–7780).

PRIVATE TAXI: **AvantGarde Cellular Transport** offers comfy cars and courteous drivers. Service is priced to compete with city hacks for those dreary trips to the airport and the Automall—and the cars are comfortable (662–5504).

REPRODUCTION HARDWARE: Do-it-yourselfers will find a veritable supermarket of solid-brass plumbing and cabinet hardware, with knobs of virtually every variety, at **The Antique Hardware Store**. Call for a catalog if you don't get to upper Bucks

Tim Judge poses outside his shop, The Antique Hardware Store.

County very often (9730 Route 611, Kintnersville, 1–800–422–9982).

RETRO PARTY VENUE: Rent the perfectly preserved vintage drugstore **Phantom Fountain**, for a *Happy Days* soda-jerk blowout catered by '50's fooderie Momi. And no, the props are not for sale (339 South 21st Street, 985–4067).

ROSES: Ravishing arrangements from **George Baker**, the ultimate in floral pulchritude (1607 Latimer Street, 545–8448).

SHOE REPAIR: Lost a heel climbing the stairs to Le Bec-Fin's bar? Worn out your Doc Martens in the mosh pit? **Benjamin's Shoe & Handbag Repair** replaces heels and soles of all sorts, from flat-footed Birkenstock, Vibram and Rockport to the loftiest of high heels (9th and Sansom Streets, 625–0444).

TAILOR: **Frank Ventresca** can create a tux that's a double-take for the pricier Italian designer version, or alter a staid suit to a more current style (315 Old York Road, Jenkintown, 576–1178).

TASTYKAKE DELIVERY: A big, checked carton containing all the Krimpets, cupcakes and Kandykakes a nostalgic Philadelphian can consume is the ultimate gift for city emigres. Select the best packaged assortment, depending on the level of addiction (1–800–33–TASTY).

UMBRELLA REPAIR: Come in from the rain at **S. Frankford & Sons**, in a tiny shop under the El. These folks will repair anything from a turn-of-the-century parasol to a gigantic beach umbrella (7416 Frankford Avenue, 333–3405).

WATCH REPAIR: Cluttered with spare parts and layered in dust, **Raykin Watch Repair** in Chinatown is a piece of vintage Philly, with a cranky staff who can fix anything from Grandpa's pocket watch to Mom's tacky Franklin Mint timepiece (60 North 9th Street, 925–8553).

WAY TO WAIT FOR A TRAIN: **Listen Up AudioBooks,** with 5,000 books on tape in stock for sale or rent, and the membership is free (1507 Chestnut Street, 568–7255).

Rooms at the Top:
Hotels and Inns

ACCOMMODATIONS NEAR THE CONVENTION CENTER: With 1,200 rooms, the new **Philadelphia Marriott** soars 23 stories above the city, and connects to the Convention Center via a skywalk. It features the state's largest grand ballroom, a handsome health club and a surprisingly toothsome cheesesteak at Allie's American Grille and Patio, one of the two hotel restaurants (1201 Market Street, 972–6700).

BATHROOMS, PUBLIC: The **Four Seasons Hotel'**s provide perfect sanctuary from the world, with every nicety one could hope for in a loo, plus plenty of room. Just try not to forget what you're there for (1 Logan Square, North 18th Street and Benjamin Franklin Parkway, 963–1500).

BATHROOMS, PRIVATE: At the **Rittenhouse Hotel and Condominiums**, the rooms are plush

> Designed in 1889, The Gables is a cozy bed and breakfast with 16 rooms and period furnishings.

and comfy, but it's the bathroom you won't want to leave—a cool expanse of marble and mirrors, perfect for steamy phone calls (210 West Rittenhouse Square between Walnut and Locust Streets, 546–9000).

BED AND BREAKFAST INN, HISTORIC DISTRICT: Despite its proximity to the stately halls of democracy, the **Thomas Bond House** has a gracious European feel and a lived-in air of pure comfort (129 South 2nd Street, 923–8523).

BED AND BREAKFAST INN, MIDCITY: What was it like to live in a 19th-century row house off Rittenhouse Square? Experience it, albeit much more comfortably, at cozy little **Bag & Baggage Bed & Breakfast**. The three-room hostelry is conveniently situated for shopping, too (338 South 19th Street, 546–3807).

BED AND BREAKFAST INN, UNIVERSITY CITY: Perfect for fussy parents visiting their offspring at Penn, **The Gables** is a handsome Victorian restoration with a welcoming porch and well-tended gardens (4520 Chester Avenue, 662–1921).

HOTEL NEAR THE HISTORIC DISTRICT: Small, discreet and elegant, the **Omni Hotel at Independence Park** boasts many guest rooms overlooking the tranquil patchwork of green park. Its lobby is a gleaming oasis of shiny brass, Oriental rugs and gilt-framed mirrors (401 Chestnut Street, 925–0000).

LOBBY: There's a '20's elegance clinging to the grand public spaces at the **Warwick Hotel**. As is often the case with hostelries, both modern and contemporary, the swell lobby is by far the finest room in the entire place (1701 Locust Street, 735–6000).

The posh and plush lobby at the Warwick Hotel.

MAIN LINE HOTEL: Conveniently situated for business travelers to the big pharmaceutical companies nearby, the **Radnor Hotel** has a solid reputation, good housekeeping and a convivial bar with lots of wines by the glass. It may not be romantic, but what's a business hotel for? (591 East Lancaster Avenue, St. Davids, 610–688–5800).

PET'S CHOICE: The **Rittenhouse Hotel and Condominiums** was Lassie's preferred hotel (yes, *that* Lassie). Its kitchen staff doesn't blink an eye when asked to boil a chopped chicken or cook up any other special repast requested by a traveler's furry companion (210 West Rittenhouse Square between Walnut and Locust Streets, 546–9000).

ROOM SERVICE: Because the **Four Seasons Hotel** restaurants are arguably some the best restaurants, period, it stands to reason that the room service meets the same lofty standards (1 Logan Square, North 18th Street and Benjamin Franklin Parkway, 963–1500).

SMALL HOTEL: The **Penn's View Inn**, a charming little hostelry by the Delaware with no corporate affiliation—only the tireless Sena family, who also operate the Panorama restaurant downstairs and La Famiglia, the nearby, big-ticket eatery (14 North Front Street, 922–7600).

TWIST ON TEA: When the weather gets warm, the **Ritz-Carlton Hotel**'s afternoon tea puts the chill on, with fresh fruit soups, elegant ice creams and just-baked cookies. To drink, there's iced coffee, cappuccino and latte. And tea, of course (Liberty Place, 17th and Chestnut Street, 563–1600).

Index

INDEX

Picture Credits

About the Editor

JANET BUKOVINSKY TEACHER is a Senior Editor at *Philadelphia Magazine* and has received a National Magazine Award for her work there. She also has written for *The New York Times Magazine, Self* and *Los Angeles Times Magazine*, and she is the editor of *Women of Words*, a book of literary biographies.

Notes

Notes

Notes

Notes

Notes

Notes

Notes

Notes